P9-DXI-158

OPPOSING
VIEWPOINTS®
SERIES

America's Prisons

Other Books of Related Interest:

Opposing Viewpoints Series

Community Policing

Gun Violence

Organized Crime

Police Brutality

At Issue Series

Alternative Prisons

Guns and Crime

Minorities and the Law

Current Controversies Series

Cybercrime

Death Penalty

Gangs

Racial Profiling

"Congress shall make no law ... abridging the freedom of speech, or of the press."

First Amendment to the US Constitution

The basic foundation of our democracy is the First Amendment guarantee of freedom of expression. The Opposing Viewpoints series is dedicated to the concept of this basic freedom and the idea that it is more important to practice it than to enshrine it.

America's Prisons

Jack Lasky, Book Editor

GREENHAVEN PRESS
A part of Gale, Cengage Learning

GALE
CENGAGE Learning®

Farmington Hills, Mich • San Francisco • New York • Waterville, Maine
Meriden, Conn • Mason, Ohio • Chicago

GALE
CENGAGE Learning

Judy Galens, *Manager, Frontlist Acquisitions*

LIBRARY OF CONGRESS CATALOGING-IN-PUBLICATION DATA

America's prisons (Greenhaven Press)
  America's prisons / Jack Lasky, book editor.
    pages cm. -- (Opposing viewpoints)
  Includes bibliographical references and index.
  ISBN 978-0-7377-7536-5 (hardcover) -- ISBN 978-0-7377-7537-2 (pbk.)
  1. Prisons--United States. 2. Imprisonment--United States. 3. Alternatives to imprisonment--United States. 4. Criminals--Rehabilitation--United States. 5. Criminal justice, Administration of--United States. I. Lasky, Jack, editor. II. Title.
  HV9471.A49 2016
  365'.973--dc23
                                                                    2015021383

b086 9251   2/16

Printed in Mexico
1 2 3 4 5 6 7 19 18 17 16 15

Contents

Chapter 3: Are Prisoners Treated Humanely?

Why Consider Opposing Viewpoints?

> *"The only way in which a human being can make some approach to knowing the whole of a subject is by hearing what can be said about it by persons of every variety of opinion and studying all modes in which it can be looked at by every character of mind. No wise man ever acquired his wisdom in any mode but this."*
>
> John Stuart Mill

In our media-intensive culture it is not difficult to find differing opinions. Thousands of newspapers and magazines and dozens of radio and television talk shows resound with differing points of view. The difficulty lies in deciding which opinion to agree with and which "experts" seem the most credible. The more inundated we become with differing opinions and claims, the more essential it is to hone critical reading and thinking skills to evaluate these ideas. Opposing Viewpoints books address this problem directly by presenting stimulating debates that can be used to enhance and teach these skills. The varied opinions contained in each book examine many different aspects of a single issue. While examining these conveniently edited opposing views, readers can develop critical thinking skills such as the ability to compare and contrast authors' credibility, facts, argumentation styles, use of persuasive techniques, and other stylistic tools. In short, the Opposing Viewpoints Series is an ideal way to attain the higher-level thinking and reading skills so essential in a culture of diverse and contradictory opinions.

In addition to providing a tool for critical thinking, Opposing Viewpoints books challenge readers to question their own strongly held opinions and assumptions. Most people form their opinions on the basis of upbringing, peer pressure, and personal, cultural, or professional bias. By reading carefully balanced opposing views, readers must directly confront new ideas as well as the opinions of those with whom they disagree. This is not to argue simplistically that everyone who reads opposing views will—or should—change his or her opinion. Instead, the series enhances readers' understanding of their own views by encouraging confrontation with opposing ideas. Careful examination of others' views can lead to the readers' understanding of the logical inconsistencies in their own opinions, perspective on why they hold an opinion, and the consideration of the possibility that their opinion requires further evaluation.

Evaluating Other Opinions

To ensure that this type of examination occurs, Opposing Viewpoints books present all types of opinions. Prominent spokespeople on different sides of each issue as well as well-known professionals from many disciplines challenge the reader. An additional goal of the series is to provide a forum for other, less known, or even unpopular viewpoints. The opinion of an ordinary person who has had to make the decision to cut off life support from a terminally ill relative, for example, may be just as valuable and provide just as much insight as a medical ethicist's professional opinion. The editors have two additional purposes in including these less known views. One, the editors encourage readers to respect others' opinions—even when not enhanced by professional credibility. It is only by reading or listening to and objectively evaluating others' ideas that one can determine whether they are worthy of consideration. Two, the inclusion of such viewpoints encourages the important critical thinking skill of objectively evaluating an author's credentials and bias. This evaluation will illuminate an author's reasons for taking a particular stance on an issue and will aid in readers' evaluation of the author's ideas.

It is our hope that these books will give readers a deeper understanding of the issues debated and an appreciation of the complexity of even seemingly simple issues when good and honest people disagree. This awareness is particularly important in a democratic society such as ours in which people enter into public debate to determine the common good. Those with whom one disagrees should not be regarded as enemies but rather as people whose views deserve careful examination and may shed light on one's own.

Thomas Jefferson once said that "difference of opinion leads to inquiry, and inquiry to truth." Jefferson, a broadly educated man, argued that "if a nation expects to be ignorant and free . . . it expects what never was and never will be." As individuals and as a nation, it is imperative that we consider the opinions of others and examine them with skill and discernment. The Opposing Viewpoints series is intended to help readers achieve this goal.

David L. Bender and Bruno Leone,
Founders

Introduction

"Both in raw numbers and by percentage of the population, the United States has the most prisoners of any developed country in the world—and it has the largest total prison population of any nation."

—Nicole Flatow,
"The United States Has the Largest Prison Population in the World— and It's Growing," Think Progress, *September 17, 2014*

A s a country founded on the principles of freedom and democracy, the question of how best to punish and rehabilitate criminals is one that has long plagued the United States. In fact, the history of America's prisons dates all the way back to the Revolutionary era, when the colonies first sought to claim their independence from Great Britain. As America struggled to win its freedom from tyranny, many of its major cities struggled to deal with increased crime and the failure of traditional methods of criminal justice such as corporal punishment and forced public labor. By the 1760s, it was clear that a new approach was needed. In Philadelphia, enlightened thinkers such as Dr. Benjamin Rush championed the idea of embracing imprisonment as a means of cultivating penitence among wrongdoers. Their efforts led to the construction of many of America's first urban prisons, including the Walnut Street Prison in Philadelphia and Newgate Prison in New York. Initially, these prisons met with notable success. Because they were located within America's largest urban communities, early prisons not only served as a means of isolating the least desirable members of society but also yielded economic benefits by providing a cheap source of labor for local merchants and businesses. Eventually, however, the public soured on this approach, as prison labor cut into the profits of craftsmen and mechanics, and housing prisoners became an increasingly dangerous proposition. By the 1830s, most states shifted to building prisons away from their primary urban centers and nearer to their smaller capital cities.

The evolution of the American prison system continued in the years following the Civil War. In the South, many states embraced prison farms, racist Jim Crow laws, and a convict-leasing system so as to create a source of cheap agricultural labor in the absence of slavery. In the North, meanwhile, industrialization and increasing urban growth led to burgeoning prison populations and the need for various types of prison reform. Some of these reforms included the establishment of separate women's and juvenile prisons. These measures were designed to offer special protection to those often seen as the most vulnerable inmates. Specifically, reformers believed creating separate prison facilities for women would save females from sexual victimization behind bars and give them a better chance to restore their social standing. Similarly, reformers also supported the construction of juvenile prisons because such structures isolated miscreant boys from hardened criminals and provided a better opportunity for rehabilitation of young offenders.

Over the course of the twentieth century, the focus of America's prisons gradually turned from punishment to rehabilitation. In the 1920s, the prison population surged thanks to the enactment of Prohibition. With more prisoners to house, a prison construction boom quickly ensued. Further, because Prohibition led to widespread interstate trafficking orchestrated by various organized crime syndicates, the number of federal prisoners also grew. This, in turn, necessitated the establishment of the Federal Bureau of Prisons in the 1930s, which, along with policies created as part of Franklin D.

Roosevelt's New Deal program, brought about various key reforms in the federal prison system. After World War II, many of these reforms also began to be adopted by state prisons. As a result, by mid-century many prisons became "correctional institutions," where inmates were allowed access to educational resources, psychological counseling, and expanded recreational opportunities in hopes that such offerings would increase their likelihood of eventually making a successful return to society. The effectiveness of such programs was somewhat negated, however, by the changing demographics of America's cities. With African Americans, Latinos, and other minority groups beginning to dominate the urban environment, prison rehabilitation programs, which provided little help for inmates returning to low-income neighborhoods, increasingly failed to achieve success. In the 1970s and 1980s, this, as well as an increased focus on prosecuting drug-related crimes and other factors, led to a dramatic increase in the size of the prison population that continues to plague America's prisons into the twenty-first century.

Opposing Viewpoints: America's Prisons examines rampant prison overcrowding and other issues in chapters titled "What Problems Do America's Prisons Face?," "Who Is in America's Prisons?," "Are Prisoners Treated Humanely?," and "Do Prison Alternatives Work?" The questions surrounding the racial makeup of prison populations, the treatment of prisoners, and the effectiveness of prison alternatives remain subjects of intense scrutiny and vigorous debate between people on all sides of the issues concerning America's correctional facilities.

OPPOSING
VIEWPOINTS®
SERIES

CHAPTER 1

What Problems Do America's Prisons Face?

Chapter Preface

America's prison population has surged to epidemic proportions in recent years. Around the nation, correctional facilities are struggling to cope with severe overcrowding and a near constant influx of new inmates. The trend toward mass incarceration has led America's criminal justice system to a veritable breaking point. Undoubtedly, something will soon need to be done to address this situation.

Finding a solution to America's prison problem begins with understanding its cause. In their search for answers, experts have arrived at a number of different possible explanations for how America's prisons have become so severely overcrowded. Some have laid the blame on race, suggesting that latent racism in the criminal justice system has landed an inordinate number of African Americans and other minorities behind bars. Others have pointed to prison privatization, arguing that private prisons have intentionally encouraged the idea of mass incarceration in order to boost their profits. Perhaps the most cited cause of the prison problem, however, is the war on drugs.

In the 1970s and 1980s, many Americans became addicted to drugs. As more and more people experimented with drugs such as marijuana, cocaine, and heroin, many cities became havens for drug users and dealers. The sale of drugs became a multimillion-dollar business that further fueled the country's growing drug problem. When Americans eventually began to realize the depths of the addiction, the drug crisis became a political issue. Hoping to clean up their neighborhoods and get drugs off the streets, many voters enthusiastically supported political candidates and elected officials who promised to crack down on drugs and other crimes. Often, these officials championed stringent drug laws that included an increased emphasis on imprisonment and long mandatory minimum sentences. While such policies may have enjoyed some initial success, they ultimately led to a dramatic increase in America's inmate population. To this day, sentencing guidelines developed as part of the war on drugs continue to result in long prison sentences for people who have committed nonviolent crimes. For this reason, the war on drugs remains one of the most likely causes of America's prison overcrowding problem.

Whether it stems from the war on drugs, racism, privatization, or some other cause, there is little question that the current prison boom presents a serious challenge that must be addressed. Today's severely overcrowded prisons are often extremely dangerous for those who find themselves serving time.

The following chapter examines overcrowding and other problems plaguing the American prison system. The authors of the viewpoints present varying opinions on what can be done, since finding solutions to America's prison problems is of paramount importance.

> "Mass incarceration in the United States
> has ... emerged as a comprehensive
> and well-disguised system of racialized
> social control that functions in a man-
> ner strikingly similar to Jim Crow."

The New Jim Crow

Michelle Alexander

In the following viewpoint, Michelle Alexander argues that the overcrowding of American prisons is the result of latent racism in the justice system. Specifically, she contends that the justice system's war on drugs has unfairly targeted minorities to the point that African Americans and other minorities have effectively become second-class citizens. Alexander is an associate professor at the Moritz College of Law at the Ohio State University. She is also the author of The New Jim Crow: Mass Incarceration in an Age of Colorblindness.

As you read, consider the following questions:

1. According to the author, how many African Americans were incarcerated in the United States at the time the viewpoint was written?

2. According to the viewpoint, how is the incarceration rate related to the crime rate?

3. What did Justice Thurgood Marshall say about the drug war and the Fourth Amendment in his *Skinner v. Railway Labor Executives' Association* dissenting opinion?

The first time I encountered the idea that our criminal-justice system functions much like a racial caste system, I dismissed the notion. It was more than 10 years ago in Oakland when I was rushing to catch the bus and spotted a bright orange sign stapled to a telephone pole. It screamed in large, bold print: "The Drug War is the New Jim Crow." I scanned the text of the flyer and then muttered something like, "Yeah, the criminal-justice system is racist in many ways, but making such an absurd comparison doesn't help. People will just think you're crazy." I then hopped on the bus and headed to my new job as director of the racial justice project for the American Civil Liberties Union of Northern California.

What a difference a decade makes. After years of working on issues of racial profiling, police brutality, and drug-law enforcement in poor communities of color as well as working with former inmates struggling to "re-enter" a society that never seemed to have much use for them, I began to suspect that I was wrong about the criminal-justice system. It was not just another institution infected with racial bias but a different beast entirely. The activists who posted the sign on the telephone pole were not crazy, nor were the smattering of lawyers and advocates around the country who were beginning to connect the dots between our current system of mass incarceration and earlier forms of racial control. Quite belatedly, I came to see that mass incarceration in the United States has, in fact, emerged as a comprehensive and well-disguised system of racialized social control that functions in a manner strikingly similar to Jim Crow.

What has changed since the collapse of Jim Crow has less to do with the basic structure of our society than with the language we use to justify severe inequality. In the era of colorblindness, it is no longer socially permissible to use race, explicitly, as justification for discrimination, exclusion, or social contempt. Rather, we use our criminal-justice system to associate criminality with people of color and then engage in the prejudiced practices we supposedly left behind. Today, it is legal to discriminate against ex-offenders in ways it was once legal to discriminate against African Americans. Once you're labeled a felon, depending on the state you're in, the old forms of discrimination—employment discrimination, housing discrimination, denial of the right to vote, and exclusion from jury service—are suddenly legal. As a criminal, you have scarcely more rights and arguably less respect than a black man living in Alabama at the height of Jim Crow. We have not ended racial caste in America; we have merely redesigned it.

More than two million African Americans are currently under the control of the criminal-justice system—in prison or jail, on probation or parole. During the past few decades, millions more have cycled in and out of the system; indeed, nearly 70 percent of people released from prison are re-arrested within three years. Most people appreciate that millions of African Americans were locked into a second-class status during slavery and Jim Crow, and that these earlier systems of racial control created a legacy of political, social, and economic inequality that our nation is still struggling to overcome. Relatively few, however, seem to appreciate that millions of African Americans are subject to a new system of control—mass incarceration—which also has a devastating effect on families and communities. The harm is greatly intensified when prisoners are released. As criminologist Jeremy Travis has observed, "In this brave new world, punishment for the original offense is no longer enough; one's debt to society is never paid."

The scale of incarceration-related discrimination is astonishing. Ex-offenders are routinely stripped of essential rights.

Current felon-disenfranchisement laws bar 13 percent of African American men from casting a vote, thus making mass incarceration an effective tool of voter suppression—one reminiscent of the poll taxes and literacy tests of the Jim Crow era. Employers routinely discriminate against an applicant based on criminal history, as do landlords. In most states, it is also legal to make ex-drug offenders ineligible for food stamps. In some major urban areas, if you take into account prisoners— who are excluded from poverty and unemployment statistics, thus masking the severity of black disadvantage—more than half of working-age African American men have criminal records and are thus subject to legalized discrimination for the rest of their lives. In Chicago, for instance, nearly 80 percent of working-age African American men had criminal records in 2002. These men are permanently locked into an inferior, second-class status, or caste, by law and custom.

The official explanation for this is crime rates. Our prison population increased sevenfold in less than 30 years, going from about 300,000 to more than 2 million, supposedly due to rising crime in poor communities of color.

Crime rates, however, actually have little to do with incarceration rates. Crime rates have fluctuated during the past 30 years and today are at historical lows, but incarceration rates have consistently soared. Most sociologists and criminologists today will acknowledge that crime rates and incarceration rates have moved independently of each other; incarceration rates have skyrocketed regardless of whether crime has gone up or down in any particular community or in the nation as a whole.

What caused the unprecedented explosion in our prison population? It turns out that the activists who posted the sign on the telephone pole were right: The "war on drugs" is the single greatest contributor to mass incarceration in the United States. Drug convictions accounted for about two-thirds of the

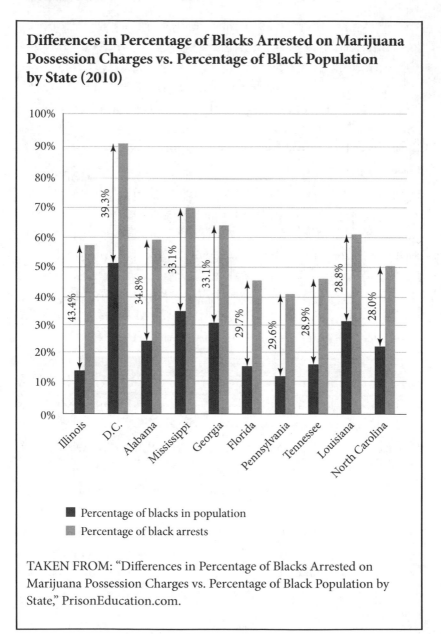

Differences in Percentage of Blacks Arrested on Marijuana Possession Charges vs. Percentage of Black Population by State (2010)

■ Percentage of blacks in population
■ Percentage of black arrests

TAKEN FROM: "Differences in Percentage of Blacks Arrested on Marijuana Possession Charges vs. Percentage of Black Population by State," PrisonEducation.com.

increase in the federal prison system and more than half of the increase in the state prison system between 1985 and 2000—the period of the U.S. penal system's most dramatic expansion.

Contrary to popular belief, the goal of this war is not to root out violent offenders or drug kingpins. In 2005, for example, four out of five drug arrests were for possession, while only one out of five were for sales. A 2007 report from the Sentencing Project found that most people in state prison for drug offenses had no history of violence or significant selling activity. Nearly 80 percent of the increase in drug arrests in the 1990s, when the drug war peaked, could be attributed to possession of marijuana, a substance less harmful than alcohol or tobacco and at least as prevalent in middle-class white communities and on college campuses as in poor communities of color.

The drug war, though, has been waged almost exclusively in poor communities of color, despite the fact that studies consistently indicate that people of all races use and sell illegal drugs at remarkably similar rates. This is not what one would guess by peeking inside our nation's prisons and jails, which are overflowing with black and brown drug offenders. In 2000, African Americans made up 80 percent to 90 percent of imprisoned drug offenders in some states.

The extraordinary racial disparities in our criminal-justice system would not exist today but for the complicity of the United States Supreme Court. In the failed war on drugs, our Fourth Amendment protections against unreasonable searches and seizures have been eviscerated. Stop-and-frisk operations in poor communities of color are now routine; the arbitrary and discriminatory police practices the framers aimed to prevent are now commonplace. Justice Thurgood Marshall, in a strident dissent in the 1989 case of *Skinner v. Railway Labor Executives' Association*, felt compelled to remind the court that there is "no drug exception" to the Fourth Amendment. His reminder was in vain. The Supreme Court had begun steadily unraveling Fourth Amendment protections against stops, interrogations, and seizures in bus stops, train stations, schools, workplaces, airports, and on sidewalks in a series of cases starting in the early 1980s. These aggressive sweep tactics in poor communities of color are now as accepted as separate water fountains were several decades ago.

If the system is as rife with conscious and unconscious bias, many people often ask, why aren't more lawsuits filed? Why not file class-action lawsuits challenging bias by the police or prosecutors? Doesn't the Fourteenth Amendment guarantee equal protection of the law?

What many don't realize is that the Supreme Court has ruled that in the absence of conscious, intentional bias—tantamount to an admission or a racial slur—you can't present allegations of race discrimination in the criminal-justice system. These rulings have created a nearly insurmountable hurdle, as law-enforcement officials know better than to admit racial bias out loud, and much of the discrimination that pervades this system is rooted in unconscious racial stereotypes, or "hunches" about certain types of people that come down to race. Because these biases operate unconsciously, the only proof of bias is in the outcomes: how people of different races are treated. The Supreme Court, however, has ruled that no matter how severe the racial disparities, and no matter how overwhelming or compelling the statistical evidence may be, you must have proof of conscious, intentional bias to present a credible case of discrimination. In this way, the system of mass incarceration is now immunized from judicial scrutiny for racial bias, much as slavery and Jim Crow laws were once protected from constitutional challenge.

As a nation, we have managed to create a massive system of control that locks a significant percentage of our population—a group defined largely by race—into a permanent, second-class status. This is not the fault of one political party. It is not merely the fault of biased police, prosecutors, or judges. We have all been complicit in the emergence of mass incarceration in the United States. In the so-called era of colorblindness, we have become blind not so much to race as to the re-emergence of caste in America. We have turned away from those labeled "criminals," viewing them as "others" unworthy of our concern. Some of us have been complicit by remaining silent, even as we have a sneaking suspicion that something has gone horribly wrong. We must break that silence and awaken to the human-rights nightmare that is occurring on our watch.

We, as a nation, can do better than this.

| *"I don't sentence people to prison for be-*
ing in certain groups; I sentence them
because they committed crimes."

Too Many Prison Inmates? It's Not So Simple

Morris B. Hoffman

In the following viewpoint, Morris B. Hoffman rebuts the argu-
ment that the problem of mass incarceration in the United States
is due to racism in the legal system. Instead, he suggests that it is
actually overly harsh sentencing requirements and problems with
the probation system that are driving up incarceration rates. He
also asserts that incarceration is a necessary part of any func-
tional human society. Hoffman is a Colorado state trial judge
and the author of The Punisher's Brain: The Evolution of
Judge and Jury.

As you read, consider the following questions:

1. According to Hoffman, how does the probation system contribute to the rising incarceration rate?

2. According to Hoffman, how should the probation system be reformed?

3. According to the viewpoint, for every one hundred thousand Americans, how many are incarcerated?

One of the common and increasingly popular critiques of the American criminal justice system is that it "mass incarcerates" our citizens. This critique often drips with accusations of racism.

A 2012 book by Michelle Alexander called mass incarceration "The New Jim Crow." But this idea that teeming racism has hijacked our criminal justice system is not only nonsense, it is also interfering with meaningful reform.

I don't sentence groups of people to prison; I sentence individuals. I don't sentence people to prison for being in certain groups; I sentence them because they committed crimes.

The disparate impact of the criminal law on some socioeconomic groups is a stark reality that requires some honest reflection—not just as to whether, and where, the system may be skewed against certain groups, but also whether, and why, those groups may be committing certain kinds of crimes at higher rates than other groups. But disparate impact is not proof of racism, any more than it is proof of group criminality.

One of the hidden truths of the criminal justice system is that most judges, including me, give most criminals chance after chance on probation before we pull the plug and sentence them to prison. There are, of course, important exceptions, including mandatory sentences for violent crimes and for some drug crimes. But we sentence most felons to probation, and most of them then serially violate their probation until, finally, we send them to prison.

Any solution to the problem of disparate prison impacts will therefore have to address not just the problem of different rates of arrest, conviction and incarceration, but also different success rates on probation.

Still, the critics are right that there are discrete aspects of the system that are driving sentence lengths too high, and that may even be the principal culprits in the "mass" part of mass incarceration. In fact, there is a large body of criminological research that shows that just a handful of criminal law doctrines—including three strikes laws and mandatory minimums for simple drug possession—drive sentences substantially higher than the average citizen believes is just. These are also exactly the kinds of sentences that are jacking up imprisonment rates.

Eliminating these overly harsh doctrines would go a long way toward solving the problem of exploding prison populations, without conflicting with our deepest notions of what is and is not just punishment.

I also believe that it might be wise to abolish probation entirely, or severely limit it, and thus to send more people to jails and prisons but for much shorter durations.

But cries to reform the way we sentence violent offenders—eliminating life sentences for first degree murder, for example—would not only not put any significant dent in the "mass" part of mass incarceration, many of them are dangerous rejections of our shared notions of what is just.

Punishment is so deeply ingrained in all of us—probably a remnant of our evolution in small groups—that every human society that has left a record has left evidence that it punished its wrongdoers.

We can, and should, argue about whether there are too many Americans in prisons, but the positions we take on that issue should not be driven by misguided feelings that punishment is wrong, that only backward societies punish their wrongdoers, and therefore that all types of prison sentences should drastically be cut back.

Politicians will not heed calls to reduce sentences for serious crimes like murder, rape and aggravated robbery because ordinary citizens in fact do not support such reductions. Even less violent crimes, like burglary or theft, often deserve prison sentences because they tear the social fabric more broadly, even if not as deeply, simply because they are more frequent.

Giving thieves and burglars a stern lecture and a free ride on probation, just because we think we need to do anything we can to reduce "mass incarceration," is a surefire way to increase thefts and burglaries.

The rule of law, just like every rule, needs the deterrent bite of punishment to be effective. In fact, maybe high incarceration rates are not entirely something about which societies should automatically be ashamed.

Part of the reason for relatively high incarceration rates in first and second world societies is that those societies have functioning governments that take the rule of law seriously.

Would you rather live in Chad, which only incarcerates 39 out of 100,000 of its citizens, or in the Cayman Islands (population 58,500), with an equivalent rate of 330 per 100,000?

Almost no one disagrees that our American rate of 700 prisoners per 100,000 is unacceptably high, and that that high rate is largely driven by our drug laws and by some of these discrete sentencing doctrines like mandatory minimums and three strikes.

But in our zeal to reform our system, the goal should not simply be to reduce the number of prison sentences we impose. After all, we could jump to the head of the class with an incarceration rate of zero simply by abolishing the criminal law entirely.

Instead, we should be asking how to reduce the number of unjust prison sentences. Asking that question may lead us to targeted reforms that go a long way toward reducing the number of days Americans spend in prison, without doing violence to our intuitions of just punishment and our commitment to the rule of law.

> *"Half a million Americans are serving long sentences for nonviolent drug offenses. Those inmates make up 48 percent of the inmate population in federal prisons."*

The Prison System Is Broken Because of the War on Drugs

Brian Mann

In the following viewpoint, Brian Mann argues that America's mass incarceration problem stems from the archaic mandatory sentencing regulations for nonviolent drug crimes established by New York governor Nelson Rockefeller in the 1970s. Those regulations, Mann states, set an influential precedent that ultimately fueled a massive increase in the size of the American prison system. Mann is the Adirondack bureau chief for North Country Public Radio in Alaska. He also produces content for National Public Radio and various regional magazines.

As you read, consider the following questions:

1. According to the viewpoint, what sentence did Rockefeller originally suggest in 1973 for criminals convicted of drug possession?

2. When the Rockefeller sentencing guidelines were first enacted, what demographic trend emerged among people arrested for and convicted on drug charges?

3. According to Mann, how did Joseph Persico ultimately feel about Rockefeller's sentencing guidelines?

The United States puts more people behind bars than any other country, five times as many per capita compared with Britain or Spain.

It wasn't always like this. Half a century ago, relatively few people were locked up, and those inmates generally served short sentences. But 40 years ago, New York passed strict sentencing guidelines known as the "Rockefeller drug laws"—after their champion, Gov. Nelson Rockefeller—that put even low-level criminals behind bars for decades.

Those tough-on-crime policies became the new normal across the country. But a new debate is under way over the effectiveness of tough sentencing laws.

'Life Sentence, No Parole'

In a little town in northern New York called Ray Brook, an old hospital and a complex for athletes who competed in the Winter Olympics in nearby Lake Placid now house inmates. One is a state prison, the other a federal correctional facility.

They're part of a massive infrastructure that sprang up in America over the past 40 years, a prison network that now houses more than 2 million people. The thing that sparked the prison boom was a new set of ideas about how communities and neighborhoods could be made safer.

Rewind to the 1970s. New York City was battling a heroin epidemic; there were junkies on street corners. The homicide rate was four times as high as it is today.

Rockefeller, New York's Republican governor, had backed drug rehabilitation, job training and housing. He saw drugs as a social problem, not a criminal one.

But the political mood was hardening. President Richard Nixon declared a national war on drugs, and movies like *The French Connection* and *Panic in Needle Park* helped spread the sense that America's cities were unraveling.

Late in 1972, one of Rockefeller's closest aides, Joseph Persico, was in a meeting with the governor. He says Rockefeller suddenly did a dramatic about-face.

"Finally he turned and said, 'For drug pushing, life sentence, no parole, no probation,'" says Persico.

That was the moment when one of the seeds of the modern prison system was planted.

Persico says Rockefeller decided that more progressive approaches to drug addiction had simply failed. The governor had heard about this new, zero-tolerance approach to crime while studying Japan's war on drugs.

"And we all looked a little bit shocked, and one of the staff said, 'Sounds a little bit severe.' And he said, 'That's because you don't understand the problem.' And then we realized he was very serious," Persico says.

Rockefeller launched his campaign to toughen New York's laws at a press conference in January 1973—almost exactly 40 years ago. He called for something unheard of: mandatory prison sentences of 15 years to life for drug dealers and addicts—even those caught with small amounts of marijuana, cocaine or heroin.

"I have one goal and one objective, and that is to stop the pushing of drugs and to protect the innocent victim," Rockefeller said.

Getting Tough Catches On

From the start, Rockefeller's policy drew sharp criticism from drug treatment experts and some politicians, who called the sentences draconian.

But no one really understood what the laws would mean or how many millions of people they would touch.

Albert Rosenblatt was a prosecutor at the time and wrote the first book detailing how district attorneys would implement the new rules.

"I don't remember thinking or believing, nor did my colleague DAs at the time, that this was going to somehow revolutionize and change everything," Rosenblatt says.

The Rockefeller drug laws sailed through New York's legislature. And pretty quickly this idea of getting tough, even on petty criminals, went viral, spreading across the U.S. Other states started adopting mandatory minimum and three-strikes laws—and so did the federal government.

But Rosenblatt says prosecutors in New York realized that the laws were doing unexpected and troubling things. White people were using a lot of drugs in the 1970s and committing a lot of crimes, yet the people being arrested and sent to prison under the Rockefeller laws came almost entirely from poor black and Hispanic neighborhoods.

"We were aware of it. I mean, it's hard not to be aware of it when you see a courtroom and when you see a cadre of defendants—many of whom or most of whom were people of color," Rosenblatt says.

Due in part to Rockefeller-style laws, the nation's prison population exploded from 330,000 in 1973 to a peak of 2.3 million. That meant building hundreds of new state and federal prisons. By 2010, more than 490,000 people were working as prison guards.

The House That Rockefeller Built

Journalist and historian Scott Christianson has written for decades about drug crime and America's prison system. He says we're just coming to terms with the impact of these policies—on poor neighborhoods, on race relations and on taxpayers.

"I think that this state and our society really has to do some hard thinking and to reflect on the impact of this long-

Nelson Rockefeller's Hefty Goals

As [Nelson] Rockefeller recedes into the recent, unremembered past, he seems an increasingly improbable figure, his surname perhaps more associated with a song lyric ("I'll be rich as Rockefeller / Gold dust at my feet / On the sunny side of the street") than with the man who, between 1959 and 1973, transformed New York into a laboratory for the ambitions and occasional excesses of government. He was a Republican, yet a missing link in the Republican Party of today: a moderate and occasional liberal who believed that every problem has a solution, and who could say, "If you don't have good education and good health, then I feel society has let you down." Such views took on more heft coming from the son of John D. Rockefeller, Jr., who built Rockefeller Center, and the grandson of that "malefactor of great wealth" John D. Rockefeller, Sr., a founder of Standard Oil and eventual philanthropist, who was once the richest man in the world. New York has had its share of rich leaders—most recently, the billionaire mayor Michael Bloomberg—but never anyone like Rockefeller.

Jeffrey Frank, "Big Spender,"
New Yorker, *October 13, 2014.*

term war on drugs—what it has meant for our society and what it has cost," Christianson says.

Cost is one thing driving this re-examination. Studies put the price tag of America's vast prison system at between $63 billion and $75 billion a year.

New York's sentencing rules were partially reformed in 2009, contributing to the closure of nine state prisons so far. Politicians in other cash-strapped states like California have also moved to slash the number of people behind bars. But most of the country still lives in the house that Rockefeller built.

Half a million Americans are serving long sentences for nonviolent drug offenses. Those inmates make up 48 percent of the inmate population in federal prisons.

Persico, the aide who helped push through Rockefeller's drug laws, says new scrutiny for the policy is overdue.

"I concluded very early that this was a failure. It's filling up the prisons, first-time offenders," Persico says. "This was obviously unjust—and not just unjust, it was unwise; it was ineffective."

This debate is far from over. Supporters of mandatory minimums say the policy has helped reduce crime in some cities, including New York, and they point to modest declines in the use of some drugs, particularly cocaine. Persico says Rockefeller himself never expressed any second thoughts or reservations about the policy that carries his name.

> "Americans tend to consider themselves
> a virtuous and generous people, and
> not a nation of grinning sadists. So why
> the urge to brutalize criminals?"

The Scariest Explanation for America's Vast Prison Population: We Want It That Way

Jakub Wrzesniewski

In the following viewpoint, Jakub Wrzesniewski examines the problem of mass incarceration and offers an explanation as to why it continues to persist. Rather than pointing to the drug war or racism, he suggests that mass incarceration is the result of society's fixation on the idea of crime and retribution as well as the deep-seated belief that those individuals who commit crimes deserve swift and brutal punishment. Wrzesniewski is a researcher and writer.

As you read, consider the following questions:

1. According to the author, how has the criminal justice system essentially criminalized poverty?

2. According to the author, why is racism not a valid explanation for the current state of the American prison system?

3. What does Wrzesniewski say would have to be done to truly correct the problems facing the prison system?

A merica's incarceration crisis is the stuff of grave, vague moral concern for many in the educated elite. We know something is rotten, on an epic scale; we know that something ought to be done; and we've internalized a few broad explanations of the phenomenon that are compelling, sensible, and wrong, in whole or in part.

The scale and contours of the problem are, by now, familiar: The American incarceration rate reached one in 99 civilians a few years ago and has now receded to one in 137. If you loaded U.S. prisons with the entire population of Philadelphia, there would still be enough bunk space for the entire population of Detroit. If you opened the prison gates today, enough men and women would stream out, trading one uniform for another, to completely staff every McDonald's and Starbucks in the country, as well as the entire U.S. Army, Marine Corps, and Postal Service.

As Marie Gottschalk explains in her largely commendable new book, *Caught: The Prison State and the Lockdown of American Politics*, the rate of incarceration is troubling because prisons abridge—selectively and in the interests of justice—the very freedom that defines America. So when incarceration becomes excessive, depriving people of liberty for no good reason, it is an affront to the liberal conscience, which for some time now has neglected core issues of freedom that are its foundation.

Gottschalk, a political scientist at the University of Pennsylvania, undertakes to describe how we reached this point of mass incarceration and why it persists, given that it seems to do us no good and costs us a great deal. Comparisons to other similarly diverse countries are as depressing as they are revealing: The incarceration rate in England and Wales is a fifth of ours, and the murder rate is also about a fifth. Canada locks away one in 850 citizens, and the frozen north is stained only with seal blood. The sole country that rivals us in its zeal for incarceration is North Korea.

Our justice and sentencing system mass-produces inmates, with little sensitivity to whether prison is the appropriate retribution, let alone effective rehabilitation. Mandatory minimum sentences remove discretionary power from judges who might otherwise be able to exercise judgment (one would think that is what they are there for) about whether prison is an appropriate response to a crime. Prisoners stay behind bars because they can't pay fees for their own incarceration, trials, or legal defense—adding extra jail time in addition to the punishment for their initial offense. This arrangement effectively makes poverty a crime. And the range of jailable offenses now includes misdemeanors that once merited no more than fines, probation, or a stern lecture from a black-robed government official. Meanwhile, American criminal justice is exquisitely sensitive to factors that should have no bearing at all. If a white man and a black man are engaged in identical criminal activities, the black man is more likely to be arrested, more likely to be charged, less likely to have the charge bargained down, more likely to be found guilty, and more likely to get a longer sentence.

Gottschalk is particularly convincing about the follow-on effects of incarceration on the vulnerable neighborhoods that contribute most to the prison population. Ex-convicts often find their basic rights curtailed. They often are not able to vote, get educational or food assistance, work in licensed professions (including hairdressing), or own guns, irrespective of the nature of their offense. Many sex offenders face lifelong restrictions on where they can live or work, as if their physical presence were as odious as their crimes. The effect is the creation of an inferior caste—largely poor and non-white—that now includes almost one in 40 people. Perhaps worst of all, locking up so many people for so little cause destigmatizes imprisonment and makes future generations of potential criminals feel that time in the slammer is not particularly shameful, and might even be a rite of manhood.

The widely accepted explanations for how this iniquitous system came to be, Gottschalk argues, are insufficient. "The New Jim Crow" thesis—best known from Michelle Alexander's 2010 book of that name—suggests that mass incarceration is a functional extension of the legacy of American anti-black racism. But Gottschalk points out that America imprisons pretty much every racial and ethnic group at shocking rates. If every black inmate were emancipated today, the prison system would remain outrageously overstuffed, and the overall rate would still be worse than Russia's. And in federal prisons at least, Hispanics have overtaken blacks in the dubious distinction of being the most disproportionately imprisoned.

Nor can we blame the war on drugs. The idea that vast numbers of Americans are in prison for smoking pot or snorting blow turns out to be a fantasy. About 20 percent of inmates are in for drug-related crimes, but those crimes are rarely limited to their own casual use. According to a 2004 estimate, only about 12,000 people were incarcerated for simple possession, without intent to traffic or distribute.

If the problem isn't straightforward racism or benighted drug laws, what is it? Gottschalk blames "neoliberalism," the system of democratic capitalism embodied by Ronald Reagan, Margaret Thatcher, and their market-loving, privatizing kin. Neoliberalism, she says, has made American mass incarceration so vast and entrenched that the "carceral state"—the politically determined penal policies and the institutions that enforce them—would need to be laboriously dismantled before the country could achieve real improvement. Neoliberal policies, she says, have worsened inequality and weakened social insurance and legal protection for the poor. Numerous elements of this system—including the private corrections industry, prison guards' unions, and the large, self-protective bureaucracies whose continued existence depends on a steady flow of prisoners—stand in the way of change.

Gottschalk's shadowboxing with neoliberalism—the bogeyman of choice for social scientists for more than a decade now, despite being such an expansive category that it can't possibly have any analytic value—is the least satisfying aspect of this book. After all, the effects of neoliberalism, when properly accounted for, probably include every aspect of modern social existence in this country. In other countries transformed by market-oriented reforms (the U.K., Australia, Canada), neoliberalism coexists with much lower incarceration rates, and hasn't resulted in an uptick in prison populations. Gottschalk's vague indictment of neoliberalism is especially unsatisfying considering that there are at least a few straightforward, functional reasons for mass incarceration, such as the fact that prison time is now meted out for more crimes, and sentences are now longer, than in the past. Steven Raphael of the University of California–Berkeley and Michael A. Stoll of the University of California–Los Angeles estimate that a third of the growth in the national prison population is attributable to longer sentences for the same crimes, and a good deal of the remaining growth comes from simply sending more people to prison (three times the number of prison admissions today per reported crime, compared with 1979). Even as anodyne and centrist a politician as Bill Clinton recently admitted, "We basically took a shotgun to a problem that needed a .22."

That's easy for an ex-president to say. Politicians still hoping to be elected have a somewhat harder time proposing solutions. Voters love a tough-on-crime candidate, and they are quick to punish any step toward loosening sentencing requirements or reducing the prison population. Indeed, they *want* our penal system to keep ratcheting up the incarceration rate.

Rather than prefer rational punishment for all, voters aware of unjust incarceration seem to prefer harsher, more callous treatment for all—a "leveling down," in Gottschalk's phrase, whereby even whites caught up in the justice system are subject to treatment once reserved for despised outcasts.

Even without leveling down, the practice of mass incarceration looks dispiritingly robust. For it to persist, it need only keep afflicting the weak and poor and feeding the greedy maws of corporations that run private prisons (and those of other amoral bureaucracies). For it to die would take a society-wide shift in values and empathy. Gottschalk doubts that concern over the ballooning costs of mass incarceration will ever be enough to motivate real, lasting change. Since such a movement would come from budgetary concerns and not moral ones, it would reduce prison rates only if it could generate savings. Unprincipled motivations are dangerous: If costs could somehow be driven down by increasing brutality and dehumanization, we might see these rise as our budgets fall. At a minimum, real change would involve making people understand the needless suffering wrought by mass incarceration; moving away from joyfully punitive sentencing in favor of punishments that reflect, to use an old-fashioned expression, the common good; and restoring the civil rights of convicts who have done their time.

In other words, we'd need a reversal of the trends of the past 30-odd years of American life. We like prison experience to be harsh. Anyone who doubts this is welcome to Google *don't drop the soap* to see the levity with which prison rape is treated. Indeed, we've countenanced, even cheered, surveillance and cross-examination of poor Americans outside prison, in the form of extraordinary barriers to obtaining social assistance, mandatory drug testing, and employers' "behavioral standards" on and off the job, the violation of which gives cause for termination and disqualifies laid-off workers from unemployment benefits. Gottschalk would like to see change that would return dignity and decency to criminal offenders, but further "leveling down" appears to be the popular preference.

Americans tend to consider themselves a virtuous and generous people, and not a nation of grinning sadists. So why the urge to brutalize criminals? Critics on the left (Gottschalk among them) like to point to America's embrace of unforgiving capitalism, but neoliberalism dominates the entire West, and no other country has mass incarceration like ours. The example of other developed countries, where economic failure and even prosecution are seen as misfortunes that can befall otherwise decent people, is instructive. There, neither social-welfare beneficiaries nor inmates are seen as parasitic failures, but as folks like us.

One dark interpretation of this discrepancy is that the struggling middle classes regard the spectacle of punishment as a reminder that no matter how bad things get for them, there are those who have it—and deserve it—much worse. This attitude can be sustained only as long as you're sure the gulag isn't coming for you next. Gottschalk's book makes it hard to believe that anyone, except perhaps the very white or the very rich, should be too confident about that.

> *"If we want to save money in the prison system while working to advance a system of reasonable justice, the answer is not to privatize our prisons . . . but to reduce the number of prisoners and the sentences they serve."*

The Private Prison System Is Dysfunctional and Cruel

Brian Magee

In the following viewpoint, Brian Magee argues that the private prison system is corrupt and harmful to the American public. He asserts that private prison companies exert undue political influence and ultimately manipulate the criminal justice system to their advantage. This, in turn, has led to unfair trials, excessive prison terms, and an unjustified explosion in the prison population. Magee concludes that the only way to solve America's prison problem is to do away with private prisons. Magee is a communications associate with the American Humanist Association as well as a former radio host and newspaper editor and reporter.

As you read, consider the following questions:

1. According to Magee, how are private prisons influencing the development of penal policy?

2. According to Magee, how are prison guard unions contributing to the private prison problem?

3. What does Magee suggest is the problem with allowing
prisons to be driven by profit motive?

A small but increasing amount of attention over the past
decade is being paid to the increased use of private prisons in the U.S. Statistics are now showing that locking people
up for profit is overriding the concept of jailing people in the
name of justice.

A recent Associated Press [AP] investigation has determined one of the causes for a sharp increase in private prisons is the rise in the number of people locked up on immigration charges. In reaction to the 9/11 attacks [referring to
the September 11, 2001, terrorist attacks on the United States],
the country made changes to immigration laws that made it
easier to detain more people and ended up being a major
source of increased revenue for the country's private prison
companies. The federal government uses contractors to keep
nearly half of the 400,000 people being held on immigration
charges. The AP also reports that "nearly every aspect" of a
huge budget increase to house those charged with immigration violations in 2005 was given to private prison companies.

There exists a "mutually beneficial and evidently legal relationship between those who make corrections and immigration policy and a few prison companies," the report concluded, adding that there's essentially no cost savings being
achieved, the main selling point used by those advocating for
private prisons. The cost to house a prisoner being held by
U.S. Immigration and Customs Enforcement has risen from
$80 per person, per day in 2004 to $166 today [in 2012], with
the government refusing to provide details explaining the difference.

According to the AP report, "A decade ago, more than
3,300 criminal immigrants were sent to private prisons under

two 10-year contracts the Federal Bureau of Prisons signed with [Corrections Corporation of America] worth $760 million. Now, the agency is paying the private companies $5.1 billion to hold more than 23,000 criminal immigrants through 13 contracts of varying lengths."

The Problem with Private Prisons

Three companies receive the bulk of the prison contracts in the U.S.: Corrections Corporation of America (CCA), the GEO Group, and Management and Training Corp. Private prison companies now house about half of the country's prisoners, up from only about 10% a decade ago. The money these companies have spent on lobbying and campaign donations is estimated to be at least $45 million over the last decade, the AP found. The result has been hundreds of millions of dollars in yearly profits.

Despite industry assurances to the contrary, a report from the Justice Policy Institute (JPI) last year indicated that lobbying efforts and campaign donations by private prison companies and their employees are done in order "to make money through harsh policies and longer sentences." Similar to the conclusion of the AP investigation about the relationship between lawmakers and private prison companies, the JPI report concludes "the relationship between government officials and private prison companies has been part of the fabric of the industry from the start."

A primary fear of this kind of relationship—a direct connection between those with power to send people to prison and the prisons themselves—has already happened. In Pennsylvania a judge has been given 17 years in prison for sentencing juveniles to a private facility in a "cash for kids" scandal. Many of those sent to private facilities were locked up for minor offenses not normally subject to incarceration.

In another instance of abuse, it was reported that CCA was charging inmates five dollars per minute for phone calls at one facility in Georgia.

It's not only immigration and juvenile detention scams that are allowing private prison companies to record millions of dollars in yearly profits. Drug users are another huge source of people to fill the growing number of private prison cells.

America's Prison Woes

In a 2008 *New York Times* story titled "U.S. Prison Population Dwarfs That of Other Nations," it was pointed out that there were about 40,000 people in jails for drug offenses in 1980, much less than the 500,000 that were currently in jail on drug charges at the time. According to the Sentencing Project, those in federal prisons on drug charges have risen from 4,749 in 1980 to 97,472 in 2010. Over half of all people in federal prisons are there for drug crimes.

The *Times* story puts the number of prisoners at 2.3 million and points out it is even more that the 1.6 million people China has in prisons, despite the fact that they have a population four times as large as the U.S. The reasons given by the *Times* for the huge numbers of people in U.S. jails and prisons are varied, but they include "higher levels of violent crime, harsher sentencing laws, a legacy of racial turmoil, a special fervor in combating illegal drugs, the American temperament, and the lack of a social safety net. Even democracy plays a role, as judges—many of whom are elected, another American anomaly—yield to populist demands for tough justice.". . .

The *Times* story points out that Canada's incarceration rate has remained stable while its crime rate has closely paralleled the U.S. For example, the average prison term for a burglar in the U.S. is 16 months while in Canada it's only five months.

In addition to investors in private prisons pushing for their increased use to increase revenues, prison guard unions

The Origins of Private Prisons

In the late 1960s, the US began to expand the powers of law enforcement agencies around the country, generating by the 1970s an unprecedented reliance on incarceration to treat its social, political, economic and mental health problems.

By calling new acts crimes, and by increasing the severity of sentencing for other acts, US citizens witnessed a "prison boom." Soon, prison overcrowding surpassed prison construction budgets, and politicians that had promised to build new prisons could no longer build them.

So in 1984, a number of Tennessee investors with close friends in the legislature recognized a business opportunity and formed Corrections Corporation of America (CCA). Their plan was to use venture capital to build a new prison and—like a hotel—lease their beds to the state in a profit-making endeavor.

"The Prison Boom Produces Prison Privatization,"
Corrections Documentary Project.

are lobbying to stop reforms that would allow for more early release eligibility and shorter sentences. If there are fewer prisoners, there is a reduced need for guards, which reduces the size and strength of the unions, providing a motivation to work against any move that would reduce the number of those behind bars.

An Uphill Battle

There are efforts to challenging the move toward private prisons and maintaining long prison sentences for more people. The national Prison Divestment Campaign, launched in 2011, is one example. It is a coalition of groups pushing to get investors to pull out of private prison companies. The campaign is made up of religious groups, immigrant rights organizations and others with a criminal justice focus. The campaign has seen some successes in getting financial managers to pull funds from the private prison companies, as well as getting other companies, such as food suppliers, from not doing business with them.

A profit motive is always going to influence public policy, which means justice and simple fairness can easily be overrun by those looking to make money, especially when lawmakers are looking out for a company's profits, not its country's citizens. With our country being a world leader when it comes to the numbers of people we put in prisons and jails, it's an obvious target for those looking to make money, the same as it would be for any growth industry. Because businesses are in place to make money for its owners, any conflict with other factors—like justice and fairness—are secondary at best.

If we want to save money in the prison system while working to advance a system of reasonable justice, the answer is not to privatize our prisons—adding the additional costs of maintaining large profits and funding lobbying costs—but to reduce the number of prisoners and the sentences they serve. It is immoral to create a system that has within it the motivation of money when it comes to taking away anyone's freedom. No matter how many safeguards are promised, the greed brought to life by guaranteed profits paid for by taxpayers will always win. The only solution is to remove greed as much as possible from the structure.

"Public and private competition ... in the provision of prison services has worked in terms of cost savings and performance measures."

Private Prisons Are Beneficial

Erwin A. Blackstone and Simon Hakim

In the following viewpoint, Erwin A. Blackstone and Simon Hakim argue that private prisons have been economically and practically beneficial. They suggest that these benefits ultimately outweigh any possible drawbacks of private prisons and encourage the further establishment of such institutions. Blackstone and Hakim are research fellows at the Independent Institute and economics professors at Temple University. Hakim is also the director of the Center for Competitive Government at Temple.

As you read, consider the following questions:

1. According to the authors, what are the reasons to use private prisons?

2. Why is competition in the prison industry beneficial, according to the authors?

3. How are the competitive benefits of private prisons realized, in the authors' opinion?

Considerable debate continues among state officials, criminal justice experts, and the media about whether contract prisons provide sufficient savings and perform adequately to justify their use. This [viewpoint] is designed to examine the evidence using publicly available state corrections cost data as the primary source.

The Necessity of Private Prisons

There are three reasons for the use of contract prisons: (1) to generate cost savings and avoid large capital expenditures; (2) to relieve overcrowding, whether ordered by the court system or required because of threat of litigation perceived by departments of correction (DOCs); and (3) the sale of a state prison to private operators for budgetary reasons.

In reference to the first reason for the use of contract prisons, cost savings and avoidance of large capital expenditures, statutory requirements in some states mandate savings of at least 5 to 10 percent in order to contract out to private operators. States, however, are inconsistent in how they measure these savings and often fail to include important avoidable costs. In particular, there is ambiguity in the categories states use for their calculations and the measurements of the state costs that should be considered for the savings required from the private operators. The states usually do not specify whether the short- or long-run costs are considered. Also, often, avoidable state prison costs are imposed on other agencies within DOCs and on other departments of state government. These costs are therefore not included in the state's calculations of cost per inmate per day. Clearly, these omissions establish artificially lower costs for state-run prisons. This [viewpoint] includes some of these often-omitted costs, provided that the sources are from state government and/or academic reports and articles.

The relief of overcrowding is the second major reason for the use of private prisons and includes both out-of-state trans-

The Need for Private Prisons

Federal, state, and local officials across the nation are facing a real crisis in their prisons and jails—too many prisoners and not enough money. Crime rates may be falling, but inmates are on average serving more time, so the problem is only going to get worse.

Private prisons can be a big part of the answer to this problem. The evidence is very strong that private prisons are comparable to government prisons in quality, and significantly less costly. State and local officials in 25 states, as well as several federal agencies, have turned to private prison operators to cope with growing prison needs, with great success. Although private prisons may not be a panacea, they are certainly part of the answer.

Adrian T. Moore, "Private Prisons:
Quality Corrections at a Lower Cost," Reason Foundation,
Policy Study, no. 240, April 2010.

fer of inmates and in-state use of private facilities. In California, for example, the courts required a timely reduction of overcrowding, which led directly to the use of out-of-state contract prisons, as California does not allow private facilities to be built within its borders for state use. Other examined states that have experienced overcrowding are Arizona, Kentucky, Ohio, Oklahoma, Tennessee, and Texas.

Whenever overcrowding exists, the statutory savings requirement is less relevant since the overcrowding must be alleviated in a timely fashion for the security and well-being of both inmates and staff. California is a classic example of the cost encountered in not avoiding substantial overcrowding. Overcrowding requires that the long-run avoidable costs be compared against the contractor's price. The long-run consideration is also relevant when the state owns old prisons that need major renovations or prisons that are subject to demolition because of age or condition, or when the state faces difficulties in raising capital.

Finally, contracting out by selling a state prison to a private operator generates an immediate lump-sum amount for state coffers. This occurred in Ohio, which sold the Lake Erie Correctional Institution to a private contractor to narrow a state budgetary deficit.

The Benefits of Private Prisons

A major finding from the cost analysis and interviews with state leaders and stakeholders is that competition yields savings and better performance across the prison industry. The economics of industrial organization demonstrates the important benefits derived from the presence of even a small competitor in an otherwise monopolistic market. In this case, even though private contractors comprise less than 7 percent of the industry, they have generated substantial competitive benefits.

These benefits emanate from two sources. First, as more contractors compete, the prices are lower, and the performance is better. Likewise, when private prisons become an available option, efforts are made by public prison managers to lower costs, and demands by employees are constrained, since public employees realize that the legislature might favor private corrections as a more cost-effective option. Further, the greater the competition, the more managerial and technological innovations are introduced in both the public and private segments of the industry. Interestingly, the authors found that in several states where both public and private contract prisons operate, there was cooperation, mutual learning of new technologies, joint training, and adoption of efficient management practices.

The Argument for Private Prisons

Our study points to a possible moderate change that could be implemented to encourage even greater competition and thereby achieve more efficient delivery of existing corrections services, which is the model of managed competition. This model was originally initiated by Mayor Stephen Goldsmith of Indianapolis, Indiana, and encouraged public workers to participate in the bidding for their services, along with private competitors, to preserve their municipal jobs. Mayor Goldsmith initiated the "yellow pages" test where he enabled contracting out of all city services whenever several providers were listed. But, he went one step further and allowed city employees to compete. By so doing, public employees, as well as private contractors, had an incentive to search for managerial and technological innovations and offer their services at competitive prices.

Adopting managed competition also has implications for the current statutory savings requirements. Where they are required, state legislators have established seemingly arbitrary levels of required savings of 5, 7, and 10 percent. It is not clear why the percentages differ or what the basis is for these numbers. The bidding by contractors often just approaches the statutory requirement and, indeed, high percentage savings may discourage some bidders and be counterproductive. It would be more effective to allow competition to determine the price. By instituting managed competition where the public sector competes on a level field with the private sector, the market determines the savings. In such a case, the complicated calculations of what cost items should be considered as avoidable costs and how to measure these costs becomes unnecessary. Managed competition has worked for many local public services, and there is no reason why it cannot be successfully implemented in the prison industry. Our suggested managed competition model is relevant for managing existing state prisons.

As can be seen from this study, public and private competition and cooperation in the provision of prison services has worked in terms of cost savings and performance measures. Indeed, public-private competition and cooperation could even be extended to further these fiscally responsible goals.

Periodical and Internet Sources Bibliography

The following articles have been selected to supplement the diverse views presented in this chapter.

Gene Demby	"Race and America's Prisons: It's Complicated," NPR, April 26, 2013.
Larry Elder	"Five Myths of the 'Racist' Criminal Justice System," Creators Syndicate, April 19, 2012.
Marie Gottschalk	"It's Not Just the Drug War," *Jacobin*, March 5, 2015.
Glenn Hamer	"Private Prisons Are Efficient, Cost-Effective," *Arizona Capitol Times*, March 30, 2012.
Nat Hentoff	"U.S. Prisons Thriving on Jim Crow Marijuana Arrests," Cato Institute, November 20, 2013.
Sophia Kerby	"The Top 10 Most Startling Facts About People of Color and Criminal Justice in the United States," Center for American Progress, March 13, 2012.
Kathleen Miles	"Just How Much the War on Drugs Impacts Our Overcrowded Prisons, in One Chart," *Huffington Post*, March 10, 2014.
Willie Osterweil	"How White Liberals Used Civil Rights to Create More Prisons," *Nation*, January 6, 2015.
Katie Rose Quandt	"Why There's an Even Larger Racial Disparity in Private Prisons than in Public Ones," *Mother Jones*, February 17, 2014.
Sarah Stillman	"Get Out of Jail, Inc.," *New Yorker*, June 23, 2014.
Matt Stroud	"The Private Prison Racket," *Politico*, February 24, 2014.

OPPOSING
VIEWPOINTS®
SERIES

CHAPTER 2

Who Is in America's Prisons?

Chapter Preface

The American prison system was designed for two main purposes: to ensure public safety and to rehabilitate those whose behavior is antithetical to normal social standards. This means that imprisonment, in addition to being a source of permanent housing for dangerous individuals deemed unfit to ever again be a part of free society, is also supposed to be an opportunity for behavioral reform for those who will one day return to society. In practice, however, most American prisons fail to adequately achieve the latter purpose. This is due in no small part to the challenges associated with meeting the specific needs of those who find themselves behind bars.

America's prisons are filled with inmates of varying race, ethnicity, gender, and age. To be truly rehabilitated into productive, functional members of society, inmates ideally need to be treated according to their unique social needs. This enormous task begins with determining just who today's prisoners are. At present, African Americans represent a large percentage of the national prison population. As such, it is necessary for prisons to recognize and address the specific social challenges that African American prisoners face and the issues they will have to overcome if they are to make a successful return to society. Similarly, prisons also need to address the specific needs of juvenile inmates so as to prevent them from drifting into a lifetime of crime and incarceration.

Another segment of the American prison system that needs special attention from correctional officials is women prisoners. There are approximately two hundred thousand women incarcerated in American prisons today. A large number of these women, many of whom have been locked up for nonviolent offenses such as drug possession, suffer from substance abuse problems or mental illness. Many are also survivors of physical and sexual abuse. Further, women prisoners naturally have different physical and emotional health needs than do their male counterparts. Some critics argue that most of today's women's prisons are not doing an adequate job of recognizing and working to meet the needs of their populations and are therefore failing to provide viable rehabilitation as intended. Others even go so far as to suggest that incarceration itself is an ineffective and harmful approach to women's corrections and that the practice of jailing women should be abandoned altogether. Wherever the truth may lie, this debate is a clear microcosm of the prison system's larger struggle to understand and meet the needs of its inmate population in order to achieve its goal of effectively rehabilitating those who run afoul of the social standard.

The following chapter examines the demographics of America's prisons, focusing on African American, women, and juvenile inmates.

| "A new study . . . has surprised a number of experts in the criminology field. Its main finding: Private prisons are packed with young people of color."

African Americans Are Overrepresented in Prisons

Rina Palta

In the following viewpoint, Rina Palta argues that private prisons are currently housing a disproportionately high number of African Americans and other minorities. Citing a study called "The Color of Corporate Corrections," she suggests that this racial disparity is the result of private prisons' selective exclusion of certain types of inmates. She also contends that this sort of selective exclusion additionally leads to poorer conditions for inmates housed in private prisons. Palta is a crime and safety reporter for KPCC in Southern California.

As you read, consider the following questions:

1. What conclusion does Palta draw from Christopher Petrella's study?

2. According to Palta, what type of inmates do private prisons generally exclude, and why?

3. According to Palta, how does selective exclusion in private prisons lead to poor prison conditions?

A new study by a UC [University of California]–Berkeley graduate student has surprised a number of experts in the criminology field. Its main finding: Private prisons are packed with young people of color.

The concept of racial disparities behind bars is not exactly a new one. Study after report after working group has found a version of the same conclusion. The Sentencing Project estimates 1 in 3 black men will spend time behind bars during their lifetime, compared with 1 in 6 Latino men and 1 in 17 white men. Arrest rates for marijuana possession are four times as high for black Americans as for white. Black men spend an average of 20 percent longer behind bars in federal prisons than their white peers for the same crimes.

These reports and thousands of others have the cumulative effect of portraying a criminal justice system that disproportionately incarcerates black Americans and people of color in general.

African American studies PhD student Christopher Petrella's finding in "The Color of Corporate Corrections," however, tackles a different beast.

Beyond the historical overrepresentation of people of color in county jails and federal and state prisons, Petrella found, people of color "are further overrepresented in private prisons contracted by departments of correction in Arizona, California and Texas."

This would mean that the racial disparities in private prisons housing state inmates are even greater than in publicly run prisons. His paper sets out to explain why—a question that starts with race but that takes him down a surprising path.

Age, Race, and Money

First, a bit of background. Private prisons house 128,195 inmates on behalf of the federal government and state governments (or at least they did as of 2010). There's a continual debate among legislators and administrators as to which is more cost-effective: running a government-operated prison, with its government workers (and unions); or hiring a private company (like GEO [Group] or Corrections Corp. of America [CCA]) to house your prisoners for you. States like California, Arizona and Texas use a combination of both.

In the nine states Petrella examined, private facilities housed higher percentages of people of color than public facilities did. Looking back at the contracts the private companies signed with the states, Petrella figured out the reason behind the racial disparity: Private prisons deliberately exclude people with high medical care costs from their contracts.

Younger, healthier inmates, he found—who've come into the system since the war on drugs went into effect—are disproportionately people of color. Older inmates, who generally come with a slew of health problems, skew more white.

Criticism

Steve Owen, senior director of public affairs for Corrections Corp. of America, one of the largest private prison companies in the nation, calls the study "deeply flawed."

In an e-mail, Owen says, "CCA's government partners determine which inmates are sent to our facilities; our company has no role in their selection."

Furthermore, he says, "the contracts we have with our government partners are mutually agreed upon, and as the customer, our government partners have significant leverage regarding provisions." It's up to the contracting agency, he says, to decide how it wants to distribute inmates and manage health care costs.

Owen does not, however, dispute Petrella's numbers.

Revealing Data

Gloria Browne-Marshall, an associate professor of constitutional law at John Jay College of Criminal Justice and a former civil rights attorney, says it's a "very interesting" study.

"What I take away from it is how prisoners are looked at as commodities," she says. "It's all about how the private prisons can make the most money."

Petrella says he used data compiled by state correctional departments, which are divided by census-designated categories and included African Americans, Asian Americans and Pacific Islanders, nonwhite Hispanics and Latinos, and essentially anyone except those defined by the census as white.

"I know these categories are fungible, but this is the data we have to work with," Petrella says.

Browne-Marshall points out that Petrella's findings don't necessarily point to a racial motivation on behalf of private prison companies, and Petrella agrees. "Profit is the clear motivation," he says. The racial component is more incidental.

However, he says, "the study shows that policies that omit race continue to have negative impacts." He says there's a larger dialogue to be had about what contemporary racial discrimination actually looks like.

Barry Krisberg, senior fellow at the Chief Justice Earl Warren Institute [on Law and Social Policy] at the University of California, Berkeley, says the findings surprised him. "I had assumed private prisons were taking a lot of low-risk inmates," he says, "that if you went to a private prison, you'd find a lot of old, Anglo prisoners. That's not the case."

Prison Conditions

This raises questions about prison conditions for different kinds of prisoners. "The rate of violence is higher at private prisons, and recidivism is either worse or the same than in public prisons," says Alex Friedmann, the managing editor of

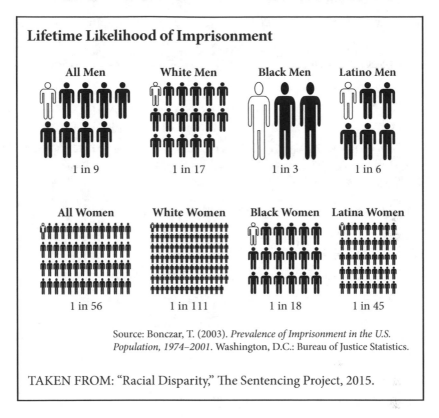

Lifetime Likelihood of Imprisonment

All Men — 1 in 9

White Men — 1 in 17

Black Men — 1 in 3

Latino Men — 1 in 6

All Women — 1 in 56

White Women — 1 in 111

Black Women — 1 in 18

Latina Women — 1 in 45

Source: Bonczar, T. (2003). *Prevalence of Imprisonment in the U.S. Population, 1974–2001.* Washington, D.C.: Bureau of Justice Statistics.

TAKEN FROM: "Racial Disparity," The Sentencing Project, 2015.

Prison Legal News and the associate director of the Human Rights Defense Center, a group that opposes private prisons. Friedmann says part of the trouble is attributable to lower-paid, lesser-trained staff used in private prisons. But some of it, he adds, may be due to this higher-risk, younger population in private prisons.

So, Browne-Marshall asks, what are private prisons doing for their age-specific populations?

"Public prisons are devoting a lot of resources to the age-specific needs of their prisoners," she says, such as building medical facilities, bringing in highly paid medical staff, and providing expensive mental health care services. . . .

Younger, higher-risk private prisoners need different kinds of services—especially since they're likely to get out of prison, back into society. And historically, younger prisoners are more

likely to re-offend, which Browne-Marshall suggests addressing with education, drug counseling, anger management and
other social services.

The trouble: While courts have intervened to require prisons to have good medical and mental health care as constitutional necessities—things that benefit older and sicker prisoners—programs that mainly benefit younger prisoners aren't
usually required. (Another reason why they're cheaper to
house.)

"How do we get corporations to do what the incarcerated
person needs when the government's not dictating it?"
Browne-Marshall asks.

That, she says, is the next question for study.

Owen says CCA offers "safe, secure housing and quality
rehabilitation and re-entry programming at a cost savings to
taxpayers. Our programming includes education, vocational,
faith-based and substance abuse treatment opportunities."
Each year, he says, CCA inmates acquire "more than 3,000"
GEDs [general equivalency diplomas].

Exclusion of Federally Contracted Prisons

In compiling his data, Petrella deliberately excludes private
prisons with federal contracts from the study. He does so because a large portion of federal prisoners in private facilities
are there as immigration detainees, not sentenced criminals.
Were he to include federally contracted prisons, the disparities
would surely be greater.

Federally contracted facilities also come with their own
baggage and civil rights questions.

Federal prisoners in public facilities, as well as state prisoners in private and public facilities, have the right to bring
lawsuits based on alleged civil rights violations. This means
state inmates in California could sue the state prison system
for providing inadequate health care. Arizona inmates in a

private facility could do the same against the private corporation that owns their prison and against the state of Arizona.

However, federal prisoners in private prisons cannot bring such lawsuits, according to a recent U.S. Supreme Court ruling.

A prisoner of this status could sue for actual damages but could not bring a civil rights suit against a private prison—the kind of suit that usually forces major changes in how prisons operate in the public sphere.

"We've gotten to the point where courts intervene in public prisons, but only under extraordinary circumstances," Krisberg says. For federal prisoners in private facilities, there's even less legal recourse, he says.

> *"Any candid debate on race and criminality in the United States must begin with the fact that blacks are responsible for an astoundingly disproportionate number of crimes."*

The African American Incarceration Rate Is the Result of African American Crime

Jason L. Riley

In the following viewpoint, Jason L. Riley argues that the growth of the African American prison population in recent years is the direct result of increased criminal activity in the black community. Refuting claims that the black incarceration rate is tied to latent racism in the criminal justice system or unfair laws enacted as part of the war on drugs, Riley alleges that more blacks end up in prison simply because they are committing more crimes. This, he says, means that a reduction in the black incarceration rate can only be achieved through changes within the black community itself. Riley is a writer and editorial board member for the Wall Street Journal *as well as a senior fellow at the Manhattan Institute and a commentator for Fox News.*

As you read, consider the following questions:

1. According to Riley, how did the Supreme Court's justice system reforms in the 1960s ultimately fail the black community?

2. According to Riley, why are racism and "the system" not valid explanations for the high African American incarceration rate?

3. According to Riley, what is the underlying problem in the black community that is leading to the high incarceration rate of its members?

In the summer of 2013, after neighborhood watchman George Zimmerman, a Hispanic, was acquitted in the shooting death of Trayvon Martin, an unarmed black teenager, the political left wanted to have a discussion about everything except the black crime rates that lead people to view young black males with suspicion. President [Barack] Obama and Attorney General Eric Holder wanted to talk about gun control. The NAACP [National Association for the Advancement of Colored People] wanted to talk about racial profiling. Assorted academics and MSNBC talking heads wanted to discuss poverty, "stand-your-ground" laws, unemployment and the supposedly racist criminal justice system. But any candid debate on race and criminality in the United States must begin with the fact that blacks are responsible for an astoundingly disproportionate number of crimes, which has been the case for at least the past half a century.

The Rise in Black Criminality

Crime began rising precipitously in the 1960s after the Supreme Court, under Chief Justice Earl Warren, started tilting the scales in favor of the criminals. Some 63 percent of respondents to a Gallup poll taken in 1968 judged the Warren court, in place from 1953 to 1969, too lenient on crime; but

Warren's jurisprudence was supported wholeheartedly by the liberal intellectuals of that era, as well as by politicians who wanted to shift blame for criminal behavior away from the criminals. Popular books of the time, like Karl Menninger's *The Crime of Punishment*, argued that "law and order" was an "inflammatory" term with racial overtones. "What it really means," said Menninger, "is that we should all go out and find the n-- and beat them up."

The late William Stuntz, a Harvard law professor, addressed this history in his 2011 book, *The Collapse of American Criminal Justice*. "The lenient turn of the mid-twentieth century was, in part, the product of judges, prosecutors and politicians who saw criminal punishment as too harsh a remedy for ghetto violence," wrote Mr. Stuntz. "The Supreme Court's expansion of criminal defendants' legal rights in the 1960s and after flowed from the justices' perception that poor and black defendants were being victimized by a system run by white government officials. Even the rise of harsh drug laws was in large measure the product of reformers' efforts to limit the awful costs illegal drug markets impose on poor city neighborhoods. Each of these changes flowed, in large measure, from the decisions of men who saw themselves as reformers. But their reforms showed an uncanny ability to take bad situations and make them worse."

Crime rates rose by 139 percent during the 1960s, and the murder rate doubled. Cities couldn't hire cops fast enough. "The number of police per 1,000 people was up twice the rate of the population growth, and yet clearance rates for crimes dropped 31 percent and conviction rates were down 6 percent," wrote Lucas A. Powe Jr. in *The Warren Court and American Politics*, his history of the Warren court. "During the last weeks of his [1968] presidential campaign, [Richard] Nixon had a favorite line in his standard speech. 'In the past 45 minutes this is what happened in America. There has been one murder, two rapes, forty-five major crimes of violence, countless robberies and auto thefts.'"

As remains the case today, blacks in the past were overrepresented among those arrested and imprisoned. In urban areas in 1967, blacks were 17 times more likely than whites to be arrested for robbery. In 1980 blacks comprised about one-eighth of the population but were half of all those arrested for murder, rape and robbery, according to FBI [Federal Bureau of Investigation] data. And they were between one-fourth and one-third of all those arrested for crimes such as burglary, auto theft and aggravated assault.

Black Society and Responsibility

Today blacks are about 13 percent of the population and continue to be responsible for an inordinate amount of crime. Between 1976 and 2005 blacks committed more than half of all murders in the United States. The black arrest rate for most offenses—including robbery, aggravated assault and property crimes—is still typically two to three times their representation in the population. Blacks as a group are also overrepresented among persons arrested for so-called white-collar crimes such as counterfeiting, fraud and embezzlement. And blaming this decades-long, well-documented trend on racist cops, prosecutors, judges, sentencing guidelines and drug laws doesn't cut it as a plausible explanation.

"Even allowing for the existence of discrimination in the criminal justice system, the higher rates of crime among black Americans cannot be denied," wrote James Q. Wilson and Richard Herrnstein in their classic 1985 study, *Crime and Human Nature*. "Every study of crime using official data shows blacks to be overrepresented among persons arrested, convicted, and imprisoned for street crimes." This was true decades before the authors put it to paper, and it remains the case decades later.

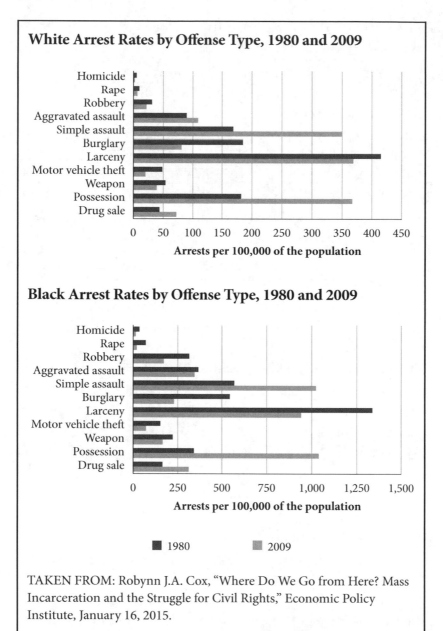

White Arrest Rates by Offense Type, 1980 and 2009

Arrests per 100,000 of the population

(Offense types, top to bottom: Homicide, Rape, Robbery, Aggravated assault, Simple assault, Burglary, Larceny, Motor vehicle theft, Weapon, Possession, Drug sale)

Black Arrest Rates by Offense Type, 1980 and 2009

Arrests per 100,000 of the population

(Offense types, top to bottom: Homicide, Rape, Robbery, Aggravated assault, Simple assault, Burglary, Larceny, Motor vehicle theft, Weapon, Possession, Drug sale)

■ 1980   ■ 2009

TAKEN FROM: Robynn J.A. Cox, "Where Do We Go from Here? Mass Incarceration and the Struggle for Civil Rights," Economic Policy Institute, January 16, 2015.

"The overrepresentation of blacks among arrested persons persists throughout the criminal justice system," wrote Wilson and Herrnstein. "Though prosecutors and judges may well make discriminatory judgments, such decisions do not account for more than a small fraction of the overrepresentation of blacks in prison." Yet liberal policy makers and their allies in the press and the academy consistently downplay the empirical data on black crime rates, when they bother to discuss them at all. Stories about the racial makeup of prisons are commonplace; stories about the excessive amount of black criminality are much harder to come by.

"High rates of black violence in the late twentieth century are a matter of historical fact, not bigoted imagination," wrote Mr. Stuntz. "The trends reached their peak not in the land of Jim Crow but in the more civilized North, and not in the age of segregation but in the decades that saw the rise of civil rights for African Americans—and of African American control of city governments." The left wants to blame these outcomes on racial animus and "the system," but blacks have long been part of running that system. Black crime and incarceration rates spiked in the 1970s and '80s in cities such as Baltimore, Cleveland, Detroit, Chicago, Philadelphia, Los Angeles and Washington under black mayors and black police chiefs. Some of the most violent cities in the United States today are run by blacks.

Black people are not shooting each other at these alarming rates in Chicago and other urban areas because of our gun laws or our drug laws or a criminal justice system that has it in for them. The problem is primarily cultural—self-destructive behaviors and attitudes all too common among the black underclass. The problem is black criminal behavior, which is one manifestation of a black pathology that ultimately stems from the breakdown of the black family. Liberals want to talk about what others should do for blacks instead of what blacks should do for themselves. But if we don't acknowledge the cultural barriers to black progress, how can we address them? How can you even begin to fix something that almost no one wants to talk about honestly?

| "One area in which the feds have fallen particularly far behind is in the treatment of female prisoners."

Female Prisoners Should Receive Gender-Specific Attention

Megan Quattlebaum

In the following viewpoint, Megan Quattlebaum argues that the specific needs of female inmates should be better accounted for in prisons. Noting that a number of state women's prisons have successfully taken steps to better accommodate the needs and concerns of their inmates, Quattlebaum suggests that federal prisons should follow suit and make the same changes. Doing so, she says, would be beneficial both to women prisoners and the prison system itself. Quattlebaum is a visiting clinical lecturer and the supervising attorney and program director of the Justice Collaboratory at Yale Law School.

As you read, consider the following questions:

1. According to Quattlebaum, how do female prisoners differ from male prisoners?

2. According to Quattlebaum, how has Iowa's Mitchellville prison succeeded at better accommodating female prisoners?

3. If the Federal Bureau of Prisons worked to better accommodate female prisoners, how would conditions improve for those prisoners, according to the viewpoint?

In the criminal justice reform arena, states have taken the lead. From rolling back harsh mandatory minimum sentences (at least 29 states have done so since 2000) to decreasing their prisons' populations (New York's declined 26 percent between 1999 and 2012, and violent crime rates fell) states are taking steps to be smart on crime.

Once a leader, the federal government now lags behind the states in criminal justice innovation. Congress has passed some laudable initiatives in recent years, including the Fair Sentencing Act, which reduced the disparity in sentencing for crack and powder cocaine offenses, and the Second Chance Act, which provided funding for reentry services. But the federal prison population nonetheless continues its seemingly inexorable rise, from 25,000 inmates in 1980 to about 219,000 today [2014].

One area in which the feds have fallen particularly far behind is in the treatment of female prisoners. In recent decades, state correctional officials and social scientists have pioneered the concept of "gender responsive" prison programming. These approaches are based on a growing body of knowledge about women in detention. As social scientists have now documented in detail, women are less likely than men to have committed violent crimes and are more likely to have committed property or drug offenses. According to a report from the National Institute of Corrections (NIC), "[w]omen's most common pathways to crime involve survival efforts that result from abuse, poverty, and substance abuse." Incarcerated women have disproportionately high rates of

The Challenge of Incarcerating Women

Women's biological needs, family responsibilities and unique paths to prison combine to create incarceration experiences that are vastly different from those of men.

While simply expanding the existing system has provided a turnkey way to deal with the influx of women inmates, funneling women through an infrastructure whose amenities, treatment options, job-training programs and cultures of control were designed for male inmates makes an already dehumanizing experience even worse.

That history can transform otherwise normal prison protocols such as strip searches, supervised showers, and physical restriction of movement into traumatic experiences.

This triggering of past abuses can keep inmates with painful pasts in a state of hyper-alertness, causing reactionary behavior that results in cycles of repeated punishment.

Melanie Deziel,
"Women Inmates: Why the Male Model Doesn't Work,"
New York Times, *June 2014.*

prior physical and sexual abuse; substance abuse; medical problems; and mental health disorders.

Recently constructed state prisons for women—such as institutions in Iowa and Washington—aim to build on these insights to develop settings that facilitate women's rehabilitation. The new Mitchellville prison in Iowa, for example, incorporates outdoor classroom space into its design. The idea, which was the result of a collaboration between landscape architecture students at Iowa State University and the officers and inmates who would live and work in the new facility, was that time spent outside could "benefit and improve the mental, physical and emotional well-being of the offenders, staff, and visitors." Washington State has put in place a new policy on gender responsiveness, and it has recognized that gender matters in things small and big: The commissaries in Washington State prisons will now sell items that are specifically suited to women's needs.

Playing Catch-Up

The Federal Bureau of Prisons (BOP) has moved in the opposite direction. The Liman program at Yale Law School . . . has released a report that describes the hardships faced by women prisoners as a result of the BOP's misguided decision to close the only low-security facility for women in the Northeast and convert it to a facility for men. Some women were sent far from their communities and families, while others were transferred to urban jails that are unfit for long-term housing.

The issue of distance from home is a particularly critical one for female prisoners. Of the 1,120 women incarcerated at Danbury [a low-security federal prison in Connecticut] in July 2013, the BOP estimated that 59 percent had a child under the age of 21. Because women are more likely than men to have been the primary caregiver before their incarceration, their absence is extremely hard on their children and families.

The question facing the BOP is whether it can reclaim its reputation as a corrections leader. The question facing all of us is whether poor, drug-addicted, traumatized, and mentally ill women should be incarcerated at all. The BOP itself has recognized that "female offenders are less likely to be violent or attempt escape" than their male counterparts, and while the solution to the problem of over-incarceration will largely be dependent upon legislative fixes, the BOP is not entirely without power to reduce its prisoner population in ways that benefit families without sacrificing public safety.

Specifically, the BOP ought to use its authority under the Second Chance Act to release eligible women into halfway houses for the final twelve months of their sentences and to home confinement for the final six months. By exercising that authority, the BOP could reduce overcrowding, improve educational opportunities for inmates, and strengthen family relationships. Moreover, as a 2012 report estimated, were the BOP to increase by three months the time that all of its inmates spend in home confinement, it could save at least $111.4 million each year.

As BOP was working to empty Danbury of women, it conducted individual assessments of the prison's female inmates and determined that a number were eligible to be transferred to halfway houses or home confinement. Indeed, the fact that as many as a few hundred women were released as a result of these evaluations is the silver lining of the Danbury closure. But this momentum toward the goal of incarcerating women in the least restrictive setting possible disappeared as soon as Danbury was empty. The BOP should conduct individualized evaluations of *all* of its inmates, male and female, to determine how many others might be eligible for transfer to halfway houses or home confinement.

As the Liman program report highlights, the decision to close Danbury to women is just one symptom of the BOP's failure to remain at the forefront of correctional thinking. The states are showing the way; it's time for the feds to follow.

> *"The case for closing women's prisons is the same as the case for imprisoning fewer men. It is the case against the prison industrial complex and for community-based treatment where it works better than incarceration."*

We Should Stop Putting Women in Jail. For Anything.

Patricia O'Brien

In the following viewpoint, Patricia O'Brien argues that the United States should stop incarcerating women and should shut down all women's prisons. She bases her argument on a similar movement that was ongoing in Great Britain at the time this viewpoint was written. In short, O'Brien suggests that modern American women's prisons are failing to adequately meet the needs of female offenders and that incarceration itself causes those offenders undue hardships. O'Brien is a writer and an associate professor at the Jane Addams College of Social Work at the University of Illinois at Chicago.

As you read, consider the following questions:

1. According to O'Brien, what type of women account for the majority of the female prison population in the United States?

2. What alternatives to incarceration does O'Brien suggest?

3. What does O'Brien say could be done to reduce the incarceration rate, even if women's prisons cannot be closed?

It sounds like a radical idea: Stop incarcerating women, and close down women's prisons. But in Britain, there is a growing movement, sponsored by a peer in the House of Lords, to do just that.

The argument is actually quite straightforward: There are far fewer women in prison than men to start with—women make up just 7 percent of the prison population. This means that these women are disproportionately affected by a system designed for men.

But could women's prisons actually be eliminated in the United States, where the rate of women's incarceration has risen by 646 percent in the past 30 years? The context is different, but many of the arguments are the same.

Essentially, the case for closing women's prisons is the same as the case for imprisoning fewer men. It is the case against the prison industrial complex and for community-based treatment where it works better than incarceration. But there is evidence that prison harms women more than men, so why not start there?

Any examination of the women who are in U.S. prisons reveals that the majority are nonviolent offenders with poor education, little employment experience and multiple histories of abuse from childhood through adulthood. Women are also more likely than men to have children who rely on them for support—147,000 American children have mothers in prison.

Prison Nation

The United States is a prison nation. More than 1.5 million people are incarcerated in the country. And this obsession with punishment is expensive. Cumulatively, states spend more than $52 billion a year on their prison systems. The federal government also spends tens of billions to police, prosecute and imprison people, though research demonstrates that incarceration harms individual well-being and does not improve public safety.

What purpose is served by subjecting the most disempowered, abused and nonviolent women to the perpetually negative environment of prisons?

Efforts to make prison "work" for women have only perpetuated the growth of the prison industrial complex. These putative reforms have helped some individuals, and possibly brought the nature of mass warehousing of poor, black and brown bodies more into focus, but the number of incarcerated people still continues to rise.

Community Interventions Work

So what is the alternative to jailing women at the rate we do? In Britain, advocates propose community sentences for nonviolent offenders and housing violent offenders in small custodial centers near their families.

There is evidence that these approaches can work in the United States. Opportunities to test alternatives to prison are increasing across the states, and some have demonstrated beneficial results for the women who participated.

For example, the state-funded project [Adult] Redeploy in Illinois has built upon the evidence that nonviolent offenders are more effectively treated in their communities by diverting 1,376 nonviolent offenders from prison since January 2011, when the program began, through the end of 2013.

Oklahoma is currently ranked No. 1 for female incarceration per capita in the country. Nearly 80 percent of Oklahoma's incarcerated women are nonviolent offenders, their presence in prison largely attributed to drug abuse, distribution of controlled substances, prostitution and property crimes.

A program that began five years ago, Women in Recovery, provides an alternative to prison for women who are sentenced for felony crimes linked to alcohol or drug addiction. The program includes comprehensive treatment and services such as employment services, housing assistance and family reunification. Women with small children are given the highest priority for admission to the program. Women who complete the program, averaging about 18 months, have a high degree of success after release.

The program coordinator has told me that 68 percent of the women who completed the program had no further involvement with the criminal justice system.

Starting with Women

Even as we learn about promising diversion programs for women, are we really ready to shut down women's prisons? If we think of abolition as a citizens' effort and believe that women should be allowed to jump the queue for transport along the path of recovery and healing, there are steps that must be taken from a feminist perspective.

We need to understand the harm embedded in the current prison system and explore what alternative responses already exist. For example, Susan Burton, the founder of A New Way of Life, a group of transition homes for women exiting prison in Los Angeles, indicates that an abolitionist perspective transforms the lives of former prisoners. Direct assistance from this program reconnects women to their families, communities and citizenship. Circle processes used by indigenous communities in the United States, Canada and New Zealand provide models for these practices.

The systemic production of mass incarceration cannot be solved simply by assisting troubled and troubling individual women. Another step to abolition requires taking the discussion beyond the individuals and communities most directly harmed, controlled and erased by the prison industrial complex to the public sphere that has passively accepted it. Put simply, we need to stop seeing prisons as an inevitable part of life.

Another Way

If we can't close down women's prisons, we can at least slow down their expansion. Efforts to isolate women from their communities must be identified and opposed.

In Denver, for example, the Fail the Jail campaign helped defeat the addition of new jail beds. Instead, the director of the state's community reentry project told me that alternatives have proven to help individual women and change community attitudes.

The case for closing women's prisons is built on the experiences of formerly incarcerated women and activists who recognize that women who are mothers and community builders can find their way forward when they are respected and supported. It is possible to imagine a future without women's prisons; whether it's achievable will require a bigger shift in thinking.

> "*Delinquency is a developmental stage, and we can either help kids through and out of it, or we can do what we're doing now, which is intervene in a way that keeps them stuck there forever.*"

The Juvenile Detention System Is Broken

Sara Mayeux

In the following viewpoint, Sara Mayeux interviews Nell Bernstein, who argues that the American juvenile detention system is dysfunctional and should be abolished. Bernstein says that the juvenile detention system is dangerous to those who enter it because it fails to prevent juveniles from returning and encourages the acceptance of stereotypes related to criminality. At this point, Bernstein argues, the system is beyond repair and should simply be abandoned. Bernstein is an author and journalist who has written two books on the penal system, Burning Down the House *and* All Alone in the World. *Mayeux is a researcher and writer on the subject of American criminal law.*

As you read, consider the following questions:

1. According to Bernstein, how do kids who are caught committing a delinquent act and incarcerated fare compared to those who are not caught, or who are caught and offered an alternative form of intervention?

2. According to Bernstein, why is juvenile incarceration a failure as a means of ensuring public safety?

3. According to Bernstein, why would even an ideal juvenile detention facility ultimately fail to serve its intended purpose of reforming troubled kids?

Last month [August 2014], archaeologists identified the first of the fifty-five human bodies recently exhumed at Florida's [Arthur G.] Dozier School for Boys—a now-shuttered juvenile prison where, for decades, guards abused children, sometimes to death, despite cyclical scandals and calls for reform spanning almost a hundred years. Dozier represents an atrocious extreme, but the failures of America's juvenile justice system are widespread. Whether labeled "boot camps," "training schools," "reformatories," or other euphemisms, juvenile prisons have long harbored pervasive physical and sexual abuse. In one survey, twelve percent of incarcerated youth reported being sexually abused in the previous year—a figure that likely understates the problem.

During the "tough-on-crime" years of the eighties and nineties, states confined larger numbers of children than ever before, with the proportion of youth in prison reaching an all-time high in 1995. Since then, the tide has turned. Between 1997 and 2010, the rate of youth confinement dropped forty percent nationwide, partly because of declining crime rates, but also because of changes in how states respond to youth misbehavior. Fueled by a mix of family advocacy, costly lawsuits, scandals like the Dozier case, and recession-era pressures on state budgets, many states have enacted reforms to transfer youth out of statewide institutions into community-based programs. California, for instance, "realigned" its juvenile justice system in the aughts [2000–2009]; New York passed similar legislation in 2012 and has recently closed several juvenile prisons, including the once notorious Tryon Residential Center.

Even with recent declines, the United States still incarcerates tens of thousands of teenagers—about two hundred of every hundred thousand kids. (State-by-state data is available here.) Racial disparities are stark: Black kids are locked up at four times the rate of white kids. And forty percent of youth held in residential facilities are there for lower-level offenses like probation violations, nonviolent property crimes, and truancy.

In her recent book, *Burning Down the House*, journalist Nell Bernstein argues that juvenile prisons should be abolished altogether. "Bart Lubow at the Annie E. Casey Foundation, which supported this book, talks about the 'my child' test," Nell told me. When reading about conditions in juvenile prisons, "we should ask ourselves, Would this be acceptable for my child if he had committed a very serious crime? If the answer is no, we have a moral responsibility to stop it. I have two thirteen-year-olds, so I think about that a lot." I recently spoke to Bernstein about her book.

A Broken System

You don't propose any reforms in your book because you say this is a system that can't be reformed; it needs to be shut down. Did you come into writing the book with that position, or was it a conclusion you came to over time?

I tried to come in with a reporter's open mind. But I have known kids who've been in this system for decades, so I did come in believing, from my own experience, that prison was a consistently damaging intervention that tended to make things worse for kids rather than better. Where my mind got pushed was when I began to delve into the research. Eighty to ninety percent of all kids, according to confidential interviews, have done something that could land them locked up. So that underscored the racial—I don't even like to say disparities—the racism of what's going on. My kid can do this; my neighbor's kid can't. . . .

If you look at those eighty to ninety percent of kids who are all committing "delinquent acts," it turns out that those who don't get caught—because there aren't police cruising their street and stopping them—or who do get caught, but are offered an intervention other than incarceration, tend to do very well. They basically grow out of it. Kids who are incarcerated, the chance that they will go on to be incarcerated as adults is doubled.

When you look at it through that frame, it's just nuts. We're taking the most vulnerable, oppressed group of kids in our country, and selectively subjecting them to an intervention that is known to turn them into criminals. The research helped me to understand that it's not that we have two groups of kids, "delinquents" and "not delinquents"—delinquency is a developmental stage, and we can either help kids through and out of it, or we can do what we're doing now, which is intervene in a way that keeps them stuck there forever.

So one issue is teenagers getting selectively punished for doing things that all teenagers do. But what about kids who have done something really serious?

I don't think they're two separate issues, because there aren't many kids for whom a homicide or a carjacking is a first offense. Almost every kid I met, including those who were in for the most serious offenses, had started out at nine, ten, eleven, usually having suffered some kind of a traumatic loss, trying to make their own way on the street, and getting picked up for something very minor. The behaviors that lead to the more serious acts are often learned behind bars.

Nevertheless, there's no ducking the question of what we do with the kid who actually endangers us. If you've read the book, I've had a kid put a gun to my head. I've felt what it means to be endangered. But it's not just my personal suggestion that there are alternatives to prison that work better: Research shows that juvenile prison recidivism rates are seventy to eighty percent depending on the state—sometimes higher.

There are other interventions, like multisystemic therapy or functional family therapy, that recognize that it's relationships that rehabilitate. So a kid, if feasible, will stay at home, but will have a caseworker who is available twenty-four hours a day with a beeper and a very small caseload. The caseworker helps to connect, or reconnect, this young person with supports in the community, whether that's services or natural supports like relatives. And if there are problems in the family, he takes the whole family as his client. Because that's another issue with prison: If family problems are at the root of a kid's delinquent actions, then airlifting him out of his family, traumatizing him, and then dropping him back into the same environment doesn't make sense.

Has any state tried this kind of program on a large scale?

Many states have tried it, but not on a large scale. Ironically, Florida, which has one of the worst reputations in terms of some specific facilities—like Dozier, which is where they're now digging up bodies—also has something called the Redirection Program, where they redirect a pretty large number of kids into these evidence-based models. But it still doesn't approach the number who are locked up.

I guess the outcomes couldn't be much worse than the current system.

And not just for the kid. As I said, I've experienced, if not violent crime, certainly the threat of it, and I don't want to ignore public safety at all. But the truth is that an intervention that doesn't work for the kid doesn't help public safety. The fact that being incarcerated as a juvenile makes you much more likely to be incarcerated as an adult counters the argument that there's a public safety benefit, except maybe for those years that the kid is gone.

Systemic Problems

In the book, you describe some horrific facilities. But you also visit a facility in Minnesota with a reputation for being comparatively humane, and you still come away ambivalent.

I really liked the warden there. I really liked the fact that when I said I wanted to see the place, he grabbed two kids who were walking by and asked them to show me around, and they were permitted to do so with no supervision. That never happened anywhere else I went. So I did feel that the kids could talk freely. There were motivational posters everywhere, and a lot of the things that the kids said closely mirrored those posters. There were more volunteers than there were kids. There were "cottage grandmothers" who baked cookies and milk. The place looks like a prep school.

But at the same time, each of these kids had spent time in the solitary confinement unit. That's something that the UN [United Nations] considers torture when used on children for any amount of time. So here was this nice place, where, by international standards, they were routinely torturing kids. Because there has never been a time in history when we've successfully eliminated the abuses that take place in these facilities, no matter how many investigations and reports and waves of reform there have been, I don't believe they can be eliminated.

But let's say hypothetically that we could somehow, despite all historical evidence, create a juvenile prison where nobody was sexually assaulting kids, nobody was beating them up, nobody was placing them in solitary confinement. They still wouldn't serve their purpose. If you think of the major developmental tasks of adolescence, they're things like forming trusting relationships, which is taboo inside any locked facility, [and] learning to make decisions for yourself, which usu-

Juveniles Should Not Be Incarcerated

Juvenile incarceration is criminogenic. Being locked up during one's youth—even when researchers control for multiple variables, *including* the offense itself—greatly increases the odds that a kid will grow up to become an adult prisoner. If all we did was follow the Hippocratic oath—"First, do no harm"—and shut these places down, it would not eliminate youth crime (unless we also offered more supportive interventions, and ameliorated root causes such as poverty, racism, substandard education and nonexistent mental health care). But given the growing body of research that tells us that juvenile incarceration fosters criminality, yes—simply shutting these places down would, I believe, improve public safety significantly.

Maya Schenwar, "'Stop Fearing Our Children': Why Juvenile Incarceration Needs to Go," Truthout, August 14, 2014.

ally involves making some mistakes. There's no margin of error inside a locked facility and you aren't allowed to decide something as simple as what toothpaste to use. They live this very regimented life where they're not allowed to make any decisions or ask any questions or form any relationships.

It sounds like an extreme version of a lot of high schools now, where the kids are very regimented and there are police on site. Kids are treated as though they're dangerous.

That's right, and what the kids who experience that learn from it is really morally corrosive. And they learn it from our fear, too—the purse-clutchers and the street-crossers. They learn that, as one kid put it to me, "Your skin is your sin." Your criminality resides in who you are, before you even do anything, and what you do is secondary. They're being told that who you are—being poor, being black, being male, whatever combination of those things it is—makes you, if not a criminal, a suspect.

Kids vs. Adults

One reason to be especially concerned about juvenile justice is that teenagers are different from adults and their brains are biologically different from adult brains. Still, some of your critiques of juvenile prisons could equally apply to adult prisons.

That's absolutely true. My first book, *All Alone in the World*, is about children of incarcerated parents, so it looks at the impact of mass incarceration on family bonds and on communities. I think that we have a special moral responsibility to kids, but I absolutely agree that prison is very often a devastating intervention when it comes to adults. And it's devastating to their kids. There's this double whammy aimed at poor kids of color who have their parents taken from them at really high rates—often for drug-related issues that would get treated as an illness if they had money—and then are themselves the target of the same system.

I should say there's been a lot of progress on the juvenile front. There's been a forty percent drop in the number of kids in juvenile facilities over about a decade. I'm also starting to sense a corresponding shift in public attitudes. When I go out and talk about this, I don't get the same kind of pushback I did with my last book [in 2005]. So I think that if we seize this moment, we might get somewhere. People are starting to ask, "Are there lessons to be learned from the movement for change on the juvenile front that can be applied to the adult system?"

Making a Difference

What can people do if they want to get involved with this issue?

Where people stand on juvenile incarceration, and on incarceration generally, has to be central to how we vote. If

people want to get involved in political activism or organiz-
ing, the Annie E. Casey Foundation has a list of organizations
in various states. There are a lot of people working on this, including groups like Justice for Families, which is led entirely
by the parents of kids who are locked up. That's a very powerful kind of advocacy. Every great civil rights movement has
been led by those affected, and I do see this as a civil rights
movement.

But there are two more things we can do. First, if you're in
a position to hire someone, think about hiring a kid coming
out of a juvenile prison. Or if you have a friend who owns a
business, advocate for that. Second, the most basic everyday
thing we need to start with is looking at ourselves and our
own attitudes, and—for example—not clutching our purses
when we see a group of black male teenagers coming up the
street. Not clutching our purses, not crossing the street. Just
checking our own assumptions. It's very widespread, the fear
of these kids. And it sends them the message that they're considered criminals and that they're expendable, that society
doesn't really need them.

> "The core 'function' of juvenile deten-
> tion in the 21st century has undergone
> sweeping changes . . . that emphasize
> rehabilitative and therapeutic services
> in lieu of strict 'punitive' measures."

Juvenile Detention Can Be Effective

James Swift

In the following viewpoint, James Swift, with the help of several juvenile detention experts, argues that the juvenile detention system of the twenty-first century is capable of providing the support and rehabilitation that young offenders need. Relying on the testimony of people who work in juvenile correctional facilities, Swift makes the argument that, despite its obvious flaws, the current juvenile detention system can have a positive influence on troubled youths and not simply lead them further into a life of crime and continual incarceration. Swift is an Atlanta-based reporter.

As you read, consider the following questions:

1. According to Mike Rollins, what should juvenile detention centers ideally be aiming to do for their inmates?

2. According to the viewpoint, how do programs such as multisystemic therapy and functional family therapy benefit juvenile offenders?

3. According to Mike Rollins, what philosophy underlies successful juvenile detention centers?

Across the nation, perspectives on juvenile detention are changing. Several experts share how they believe modern juvenile justice is implementing more rehabilitative models and what the ultimate dividends may be for both young people and U.S. society as a whole.

Mike Rollins, executive director of Coosa Valley Youth Services (CVYS) in Anniston, Ala., has been at the facility for more than 30 years. His experiences, however, aren't just limited to working there.

At 17, Rollins walked into CVYS for the first time. "I was engaged in drug use," Rollins said. "I was a teenager, and my parents, really, became aware of my activities and turned me into the police department."

After being released by the Department of Youth Services, he returned to the facility looking for part-time employment. Starting off in a maintenance position, he eventually rose to the position of executive director after working at the facility for more than three decades.

He notes the smell of fresh paint outside one of the detention center's visitation rooms. For a building built in 1974, he said, the facility is in very good condition.

Rollins' facility is divided into three primary buildings: a detention center, home to an all-male juvenile population; the Lewis Academy, a barracks-style center for non-delinquent young males; and the Attention Home, which contains an exclusively female population.

"I would say, typically, we're going to have a male youth, more often than not, [a] Caucasian," he said. "Multiple theft or assault, or maybe a little more serious, possibly. We get a fair number of domestic violence type cases."

Rollins said that the typical CVYS resident is between the ages of 15 and 17, with the average juvenile staying at the facility for "a couple of weeks" while their cases are being processed. If specific needs are required, like a psychiatric evaluation or specialized treatment placement, he said their stays are generally a little longer.

The facility, deemed by Rollins as a "publicly-funded, non-profit corporation," serves 11 combined counties in the northern and central Alabama region. Geographically, the facility serves a population consisting of more than 700,000 people.

In such a vast area, Rollins said that it's difficult to make generalized statements about the backgrounds of the facility's residents. "There's a lot of variation in some of those counties," he said. Most of his residents typically come from single-parent homes, are behind in school and generally have multiple offenses, mostly, "minor stuff," he says like truancy and running away from home.

"But we also get first-time offenders," he said. "We also get professional families' children. We've had law enforcements' children, physicians' and attorneys' children, we've had politicians' children. We've had children from non-broken families."

While CVYS doesn't track parental and guardian abuse as a statistic, Rollins said that it's likely a "fairly common" piece of what the juveniles have experienced prior to arriving at his facility.

"Whether it's physical, whether it's mental, emotional or whether it's sexual," he said, "it would be hard to guesstimate, but it's probably more than most people would imagine or realize."

The Importance of Personnel

Over the last decade, numerous juvenile justice reform initiatives have come to pass, with major implications for juvenile detention facilities. With many states turning toward community-based alternatives and other diversion programs, the core "function" of juvenile detention in the 21st century has undergone sweeping changes, with many advocates and system-involved personnel adopting policies and procedures that emphasize rehabilitative and therapeutic services in lieu of strict "punitive" measures.

Reclaiming Futures [juvenile] justice fellow Eric Shafer was the chief probation officer for the Montgomery County Juvenile Court in Dayton, Ohio, for eight years. While he believes the fundamental purpose of juvenile detention is to protect the public from young people that have committed very serious crimes, he also thinks that juvenile detention serves a greater purpose for both youth and society.

"I think you can do a lot of fantastic things in detention as long as you are serving the correct kids," Shafer said. He ultimately believes that many organizations, however, are overusing detention for status offenses and low-level first-time offenders.

"There are a number of very positive communities that are really moving forward to reform use of detention," he said, "but if I had to make a judgment, we still have a long way to go in the country."

Due to budget cuts, he believes many facilities are incapable of bringing in the best rehabilitative programs. But if detention centers "invest" in qualified and devoted personnel, he stated, there's still an opportunity for facilities to provide excellent therapeutic services for residents. "I think the key to making a detention center a positive experience lies in staff," he said. "Although a number of courts have had to cut back on staff, training and development of staff, I think, is the key in being successful when youth are detained."

Staff shouldn't just be there to "hold them down," he believes. If personnel are able to provide high-quality therapeutic services with young people in detention, Shafer said that even budget-strapped facilities have the capability to provide excellent rehabilitation services for juveniles.

Similarly, Rollins believes successful youth rehabilitative services hinge on supportive and impassioned personnel.

"You can have a structure, you can have a best practices program, anywhere in the country," he said. "You can try to replicate what people do successfully, but if you don't have the right people running or operating it, it's going to fall on its face."

Rollins said that most of his staff have been working at CVYS for years, some of them even decades. "We try to keep people, we try to train them to be better at what they do."

He believes that it is more important to "inundate" juveniles with services during detention stays than simply provide short-term housing. "We all know that a lot of these kids don't see themselves in the greatest of lights," he said. "We're not going to boost them up to feeling like celebrities, but we want them to feel like they've got a valid, strong place in the world."

New Perspectives on Treatment and Rehabilitation

"Juvenile detention in the 21st century should be about keeping kids and communities safe," Rollins believes. "The kids that go to detention need to be the kids that, if they're not in detention, somebody's at risk—either that child, or somebody in the community."

He believes that juvenile detention shouldn't be thought of as a punishment, but as an opportunity to get juveniles on the path to becoming better students and citizens.

"We understand that these teen years are really, really tough times for a lot of people," Rollins said. "If we can give them as many tools as they get, holistically, [we] stand a lot better chance of success when they leave us."

Rollins believes that, in addition to counseling and academic services, physical activity serves as an important component in rehabilitating juvenile offenders. Boys at the detention center shoot hoops at a carpeted basketball court, and residents at the Lewis Academy regularly engage in rappel tower training exercises. Many of the female residents are involved in yoga programs and participate in equine therapy sessions. Rollins is a strong proponent of horticultural therapy for adolescents—he said that the process of raising and nurturing a plant builds many of the same empathetic tendencies required to rear a child.

His facility uses a Polycom videoconferencing system—the very device used in some of his residents' court proceedings—to take students on "virtual field trips." He believes that involvement with the community is essential, but realizes there are certain challenges—primarily, confidentiality issues—that make outside interaction problematic. Even so, he notes that positive feedback from outside the facility often motivates his residents.

"We don't want to be ostracized from the community," he said.

In Montgomery County, Shafer said that juvenile rehabilitation begins before youth even enter detention facilities, as every young person that enters the juvenile justice system is processed through an intervention center, which is open 24 hours a day.

"A kid comes to us, and we do an initial screening on that young person to determine what kind of needs they may have," he said. "If they indicate they do have some need, they're going to move on to a standardized assessment that's going to tell us 'hey, does this young person have a substance abuse problem and do they have some mental health needs?'"

After being screened, administrators help young people coordinate services, either in detention or elsewhere in the community. "We're able to link that person to substance abuse treatment, mental health treatment, issues with treatment in school, whatever, they need," Shafer said.

"A lot of times, we will make phone calls, set up an appointment for them, maybe even give them a ride to get that relationship started," he said. "We lose a lot of young people in this phase, because we leave it up to them to make sure they get their next appointment."

By coordinating services, Shafer said that the model prevents many young people from "falling through the cracks" en route to obtaining treatment. Statistically, he said that young offenders have greater likelihoods of sticking with intervention services if they attend the first three meetings.

"When they complete treatment," he said, "we're able to move them on to bigger and better things, getting them into their community, moving them into all kinds of opportunities."

Building Better Futures

"I think that, from a community perspective, and particularly, the schools' perspectives, a lot of people look down on the kids that come here," Rollins said. "When they come in, there may be fear, trepidation, those kinds of things, or there could be bravado, feeling like a tough guy." He said that it's his job to help these young people come "back to reality," to show them that their stay at CVYS could be a strong and progressive experience.

"We need, as a unit, to make an impact on those kids right away," he said. "Our goal is to make sure it's not dead time, and that it's truly productive time, that we clean them out, clean them up, help them get healthier, help them get their mind stronger and help them understand their place as a juvenile in this world is to be a student."

Shafer said that therapeutic services allow young people in detention the opportunity to develop relational and social skills that will ultimately help them better interact in society. "A lot of times, young people don't have skills to just communicate," Shafer said. "As a result, they resort to violence or they treat people the way they really don't want to treat them."

Methods-based practices like multisystemic therapy (MST) and functional family therapy (FFT), he said, have been proven to have positive outcomes for those involved in the juvenile justice system. "The payoff is that you're going to have young people that are better prepared," he believes. "I don't mean that they have a new degree or training in this or that, but I think they're better individuals. They know better how to think before they act, they know better how to run back into their peers and solve problems themselves."

Rollins also said that the juvenile population is in dire need of "life management skills."

"I think it's important that we as a culture—a country, a people—help kids see themselves differently," he said. "We need to help them visualize themselves as successful, as people with opportunities for a future, as being able to learn, as being employable."

Rollins summarized his philosophy on the purpose of juvenile detention as, ultimately, a character-building process.

"What we do here is to try and teach kids that you are capable, you can be a good person, you can be as good as you want to be, you're going to get the respect that you give [and] we're going to support you if we can," he concluded.

"If there's any way we can help you become a better person, that's what we're here for."

Periodical and Internet Sources Bibliography

The following articles have been selected to supplement the diverse views presented in this chapter.

Julie Ajinkya	"Rethinking How to Address the Growing Female Prison Population," Center for American Progress, March 8, 2013.
Lily Bixler	"Women Prisoners: Gender Matters," Clayman Institute for Gender Research, April 24, 2012.
Nigel Jaquiss	"Spare the Jail, Spoil the Child?," *Willamette Week*, May 7, 2014.
Molly Knefel	"Trying to Fix America's Broken Juvenile Justice System," *Rolling Stone*, January 22, 2015.
Jerry Large	"Kids, Jails a Bad Combination; Society Can Do Better," *Seattle Times*, April 1, 2015.
Katie McDonough	"More Treatment, Less Jails: Incarcerating Pregnant Women for Drug Use Is Dangerous, Not Compassionate," *Salon*, March 26, 2015.
Anna Merlan	"Should We Stop Putting Women in Prison?," *Jezebel*, November 7, 2014.
Antonio Moore	"The Black Male Incarceration Problem Is Real and It's Catastrophic," *Huffington Post*, February 17, 2015.
John Oliver	"Calling Out America's Racist, Broken Prison System," Everyday Feminism, September 6, 2014.
Brad Plumer	"Throwing Children in Prison Turns Out to Be a Really Bad Idea," *Washington Post*, June 15, 2013.
Laurence Steinberg	"Justice System Is Failing Young Black Men," CNN, March 11, 2014.

OPPOSING
VIEWPOINTS®
SERIES

CHAPTER 3

Are Prisoners Treated Humanely?

Chapter Preface

While America's prison system has come under fire from human rights activists for a variety of reasons, one of the most common reasons is the harsh treatment many inmates endure during their time behind bars. Strict disciplinary practices, physical and sexual abuse, and neglect are but a few of the conditions from which such activists have sought to free prisoners over the years. It is the practice of solitary confinement, however, that has likely drawn the most indignation from critics.

The historical roots of solitary confinement in America's prisons date back to the late eighteenth century. At that time, there were two major philosophical approaches around which prisons operated: the Auburn system and the Pennsylvania system. Within the Auburn system, prisoners participated in group work projects on a regular basis until they finished their sentences. In the Quaker-devised Pennsylvania system, on the other hand, prisoners spent virtually their entire sentences in strict isolation. Confined in small cells with private, walled-off yards, prisoners were kept entirely separated and had no meaningful contact with other inmates or guards. Despite the fact that it soon became clear that this type of isolation frequently led to insanity and even suicide, the concept of solitary confinement persisted even as the Pennsylvania and Auburn systems were merged in the creation of modern prisons.

In today's prisons, solitary confinement serves three distinct purposes: disciplinary segregation, administrative segregation, and protective custody. As a form of disciplinary segregation, solitary confinement functions as a punishment for inmates who fail to abide by institutional rule. When utilized for administrative segregation purposes, solitary confinement is used to segregate particularly troublesome inmates from the general prison population so as to ensure that order is maintained within the facility. Finally, solitary confinement units can also serve as protective custody housing for inmates who request to be separated from the general population or who cannot be safely housed among other inmates.

Because of the extreme degree of isolation involved in the practice, the use of solitary confinement in American prisons remains a continual point of contention between prison officials and human rights activists. Opponents of solitary confinement allege that locking up prisoners in isolation for extended periods is an inhumane approach to corrections that ultimately leads to myriad physical and mental health issues. Supporters of solitary confinement, meanwhile, typically argue that it is an effective and necessary tool for keeping prisons as safe and orderly as possible. While this debate has grown louder over the years, solitary confinement units continue to have a place in nearly every American prison.

The following chapter further debates the use of solitary confinement and examines other punitive measures such as dietary restrictions and prisoner disenfranchisement used against those in America's prisons.

"It is due time that all states . . . recognize that prolonged solitary confinement is a moral and fiscal price we cannot afford to pay."

Solitary Confinement Is Torture—and Morally Wrong

Heather Rice

In the following viewpoint, Heather Rice argues that solitary confinement is an inhumane, torturous practice that should be outlawed. Citing historical criticism and scientific evidence, Rice contends that solitary confinement causes inmates such extreme physical and mental distress that it effectively qualifies as a form of torture. This leads her to conclude that the practice is both morally wrong and unfit for use in modern American prisons. Rice was the director of the US prisons policy program for the National Religious Campaign Against Torture prior to becoming the senior policy advisor for Justice Fellowship.

As you read, consider the following questions:

1. According to the viewpoint, what did Justice Samuel Freeman Miller say about solitary confinement in his 1890 opinion?

2. What are the effects of solitary confinement, according to Dr. Craig Haney?

3. According to Rice, why is solitary confinement wrong from a spiritual point of view?

Dozens of prison inmates at Virginia's Red Onion super-max prison resorted to hunger striking in order to call attention to inhumane confinement conditions. As reported in your May 24 article (http://www.ibtimes.com/articles/344860/20120524/virginia-prisoners-hunger-strike-solitary-confinement.htm), the prisoners are protesting the use of prolonged solitary confinement, which the strikers describe as 'torture.' Prisoners at Red Onion spend 23 hours a day in a cell alone. Some, including those with mental illness, have been kept in isolation for years.

These starving Virginia prisoners are not the first to identify that solitary confinement can rise to the level of torture.

In 1842, the novelist Charles Dickens visited the Eastern Pennsylvania Penitentiary and said: The system here is rigid, strict and hopeless solitary confinement. I believe it . . . to be cruel and wrong. I hold this slow and daily tampering with the mysteries of the brain, to be immeasurably worse than any torture of the body.

In an 1890 opinion, U.S. Supreme Court justice Samuel Freeman Miller made the following observation about prisoners held in solitary confinement: A considerable number of the prisoners fell, after even a short confinement, into a semi-fatuous condition, from which it was next to impossible to arouse them, and others became violently insane; others still, committed suicide; while those who stood the ordeal better were not generally reformed, and in most cases did not recover sufficient mental activity to be of any subsequent service to the community.

Sadly, we have not learned our history lesson when it comes to the damaging and ineffective results of solitary con-

Solitary Confinement Is Torture

Researchers have demonstrated that prolonged solitary confinement causes a persistent and heightened state of anxiety and nervousness, headaches, insomnia, lethargy, nightmares, heart palpitations, and fear of impending nervous breakdowns. Other documented effects include confused thought processes, an oversensitivity to stimuli, irrational anger, social withdrawal, hallucinations, violent fantasies, emotional flatness, mood swings, chronic depression, as well as suicidal ideation.

"Torture: The Use of Solitary Confinement in U.S. Prisons,"
Center for Constitutional Rights, May 31, 2012.

finement. In fact, from 1995 to 2000, the growth rate of segregation units significantly surpassed the prison growth rate overall: 40 percent compared to 28 percent.

In a 2009 *New Yorker* article that brought solitary confinement to national attention, Atul Gawande described the personal stories of several people who were subject to long-term solitary confinement, including Terry Anderson (the American diplomat held for years in Lebanon), Senator John McCain, and prisoners of war in Yugoslavia. Gawande tellingly observed that none saw solitary confinement as anything less than torture. He also noted electroencephalogram, or EEG, studies going back to the 1960s have shown diffuse slowing of brain waves in prisoners after just a week of solitary confinement.

The Commission on Safety and Abuse in America's Prisons, a national bipartisan task force established in 2006, reported that among the dozens of studies on the use of solitary confinement conducted since the 1970s, there was not a single study of nonvoluntary solitary confinement lasting more than 10 days that did not document negative psychiatric results in its subjects.

Nationally recognized expert Dr. Craig Haney, social psychologist and psychology professor at the University of California, Santa Cruz, found extraordinarily high rates of symptoms of psychological trauma among prisoners held in long-term solitary confinement in his systematic analysis of prisoners held in super-max prisons. More than four out of five of those evaluated suffered from feelings of anxiety and nervousness, headaches, troubled sleep, and lethargy or chronic tiredness, and over half complained of nightmares, heart palpitations, and fear of impending nervous breakdowns. Nearly half suffered from hallucinations and perceptual distortions, and a quarter experienced suicidal ideation.

Citing scientific studies demonstrating the lasting mental harm caused by isolation in a presentation before the United Nations General Assembly in October 2011, the UN special rapporteur on torture Juan Mendez declared that solitary confinement can amount to torture and called for an absolute prohibition of prolonged solitary confinement in excess of 15 days.

The National Religious Campaign Against Torture, or NRCAT, a coalition of 315 religious organizations that have united to abolish torture, has launched a nationwide campaign to end prolonged solitary confinement. The question of whether someone should be punished is separate from whether we should, as a nation, permit punishment that is so severe it amounts to torture. When we analyze the latter question through the lens of faith, our answer is an unequivocal no.

Our faith traditions teach us that every human being possesses inherent dignity, a quality that does not disappear behind prison gates. Prolonged isolation violates individuals' God-given dignity by destroying prisoners' minds. More often than not, prisoners held in solitary confinement return to society as less functional human beings that are more likely to recommit crimes.

NRCAT has been vocal in its opposition to Virginia's overuse of prolonged solitary confinement, including urging Governor [Bob] McDonnell to provide for independent experts to assist in the Virginia Department of Corrections' review into long-term solitary confinement. Independent review using expert data analysis methodology has been essential to successfully implementing alternatives to solitary confinement in other states like Mississippi, Illinois, and Colorado. These states and others have seen far less violence in prison and far less cost to taxpayers as a result of reforming their solitary confinement policies.

It is due time that all states, including Virginia, recognize that prolonged solitary confinement is a moral and fiscal price we cannot afford to pay.

> *"Not every felon deserves to burn in hell, but some do. If solitary confinement is hell on earth, then we should still use it for the worst."*

Yes, Some Inmates Still Deserve Solitary Confinement

Greg Dobbs

In the following viewpoint, Greg Dobbs argues in favor of retaining solitary confinement as a means of punishment within prisons. While he acknowledges the harsh nature of the practice and the potential risks to those who are forced to endure it, Dobbs contends that it is still a justified and necessary measure, at least in certain circumstances. A former ABC News correspondent, Dobbs is a journalist and professional public speaker.

As you read, consider the following questions:

1. According to Dobbs, what is the big reason for incarceration that opponents of solitary confinement typically don't mention?

2. According to Dobbs, under what circumstances should solitary confinement not be used?

3. According to Dobbs, why is it necessary to retain the use of solitary confinement?

When Colorado's new prisons chief voluntarily checked in last month [February 2014] for a 20-hour stay in solitary confinement, it was commendable. If he didn't know before his ordeal just how gutsy it was, then by the time he got out—feeling "as if I'd been there for days"—he knew it cold.

"I sat with my mind," Department of Corrections boss Rick Raemisch wrote in an op-ed for the *New York Times*, wondering "how long would it take before Ad Seg (the prison term for solitary) chipped that away. I don't know, but I'm confident that it would be a battle I would lose."

The good news is, he has drawn a lot of attention to the sinister side of solitary confinement. NPR broadcast almost an hour about the issue last week, and the *Times'* David Brooks followed up with a compassionate column called "The Archipelago of Pain."

But the bad news is this new national focus on reform risks throwing the baby out with the bathwater.

Why We Use Solitary Confinement

We have to remember that convicted criminals typically aren't sentenced to solitary; they are sentenced to prison. I've been in plenty of prison cells while covering stories, including death rows, and it's scary to feel the confinement of a 9-by-6 cage even for a few minutes, let alone a few years. But if convicts mind their manners, at least it shouldn't get worse than that. It's only when they don't—when they do something egregiously bad—that they end up in solitary.

The trouble is, in his op-ed, Raemisch never once used any form of the word "punish." Not about solitary, not even about the general idea of imprisonment. Rather, he wrote, "Our job in corrections is to protect the community." Sure it is, and we're awfully glad you do it, but that's not the whole story. Neither is the necessary goal of correcting criminals' bad behavior through rehabilitation, necessary because most felons someday will live again among us. That's why we call it the "Department of Corrections."

Yet one of the big reasons we lock up bad guys wasn't even mentioned—not by Raemisch, not by the *Times*, hardly by NPR—partly because many people believe it's not civilized to admit it: Punishment, or as some define it, society's retribution for violating society's laws.

Which brings us back to solitary: How else do you punish someone who's already being punished? One prisoner was quoted in the NPR program griping that his mattress in solitary was uncomfortable. Sorry, pal, but the man you murdered while already serving time doesn't get to complain anymore about bad mattresses—or anything else. If the punishment were to fit the crime, you'd have more to worry about than a bad mattress.

A Necessary Evil

The prisons chief is absolutely right to advocate that we shouldn't throw the mentally ill into solitary confinement; that we probably shouldn't throw anyone in, ill or not, for emotionally unbearable stretches; and that we need a buffer to allow cons recently released from solitary to decompress.

When Raemisch's predecessor, Tom Clements, was shot and killed last year, the problem wasn't just that his murderer had suffered in solitary confinement; it was that thanks to bad paperwork and premature parole, he'd gone almost straight from solitary to the street.

Which is where the baby and the bathwater come in. The bathwater we need to throw out is the occasionally arbitrary and arguably excessive spells in solitary to which some prisoners are condemned. When a punishment is counterproductive all around, it should stop. But the baby we need to keep is the penultimate punishment of solitary confinement. It's all we've got when no other form of behavior modification has worked.

Not every felon deserves to burn in hell, but some do. If solitary confinement is hell on earth, then we should still use it for the worst. They've earned it.

> "The fading of the use of nutraloaf is part of a larger long-term trend toward professionalization and, in most respects, more humane conditions of confinement."

Food as Punishment: Giving U.S. Inmates 'The Loaf' Persists

Eliza Barclay

In the following viewpoint, Eliza Barclay examines the use of nutraloaf, a special food that technically meets legal dietary requirements but is made to be as bland and unappealing as possible, in US prisons. Barclay points out that many civil rights activists are against the use of nutraloaf, which they consider to be an abusive and unfair dietary punishment. Barclay is a contributing reporter and editor for National Public Radio (NPR).

As you read, consider the following questions:

1. According to Barclay, why is nutraloaf used in prisons?

2. From a scientific perspective, why is forcing prisoners to eat nutraloaf an inhumane form of punishment, according to Barclay?

3. According to the viewpoint, on what legal grounds are prisoners fighting back against the use of nutraloaf?

In many prisons and jails across the U.S., punishment can come in the form of a bland, brownish lump. Known as nutraloaf, or simply "the loaf," it's fed day after day to inmates who throw food or, in some cases, get violent. Even though it meets nutritional guidelines, civil rights activists urge against the use of the brick-shaped meal.

Tasteless food as punishment is nothing new: Back in the 19th century, prisoners were given bread and water until they'd earned with good behavior the right to eat meat and cheese.

But the loaf is something above and beyond. Prisons and jails are allowed to come up with their own version, so some resort to grinding up leftovers into a dense mass that's re-heated. Other institutions make loaves from scratch out of shredded and mashed vegetables, beans and starches. They're rendered even more unappetizing by being served in a small paper sack, with no seasoning.

Prisoners who've had the loaf hate it. Johnnie Walton had to eat it in the Tamms super-max [prison] in Illinois. He describes it as "bland, like cardboard." Aaron Fraser got the loaf while he was serving time from 2004 to 2007 in several different institutions for a counterfeit-check scheme. He loathed it.

"They take a bunch of guck, like whatever they have available, and they put it in some machine," Fraser says. "I would have to be on the point of dizziness when I know I have no choice [to eat it]."

No one knows exactly how many institutions use it, but Benson Li, the former president of the Association of Correctional Food Service Affiliates, estimates that the number is over 100. At least 12 states—including California, Texas and New York—serve it in state-run institutions, as do dozens of municipal and county jails across the country.

In Pennsylvania state prisons, "food loaf" is made with milk, rice, potatoes, carrots, cabbage, oatmeal, beans and margarine. The Clark County jail in Washington State serves a version with most of those ingredients, plus ground beef or chicken, apples and tomatoes.

Law enforcement says the loaf isn't so bad. "It's a food source; it contains all the vitamins and nutrients and minerals that a human being needs," says Milwaukee County Sheriff David Clarke, who has used the loaf in his jail for five years. "It's been approved by the courts. I've had it myself—it's like eating meatloaf."

But prisoners who misbehave don't just get it once. They have to eat it at every meal, for days or weeks at a time. That's why it works as a deterrent, says Sheriff Clarke.

"If you're up on a first-degree murder charge, or some serious sexual assault of a child, you don't have much to lose in jail," says Clarke.

"But when we started to use this in the disciplinary pods, all of a sudden the incidence of fights, disorder, or attacks against our staff started to drop tremendously. The word got around—we knew it would. And we'll often hear from inmates, 'Please, please, I won't do that anymore. Don't put me in the disciplinary pod. I don't want to eat nutraloaf.'"

Scientists say it's the monotony of eating the loaf that's the real punishment. Marcia Pelchat, a physiological psychologist at the Monell Chemical Senses Center in Philadelphia, says humans have evolved to crave a variety of food.

"Having to eat the loaf over and over again probably makes people miserable. They might be a little nauseated by it, they're craving other foods," says Pelchat.

And it can sometimes stop prisoners from eating altogether. "It's very difficult to consume enough calories to keep your weight up if you're on a boring diet," says Pelchat.

That's why human rights advocates say it's unethical to use food as punishment in this way.

"Given that food is clearly recognized as a basic human need to which prisoners are constitutionally entitled, restric-

Recipe for Nutraloaf

During September and October 2009, nutraloaf was prepared by Aramark and provided to the Milwaukee County Jail using a recipe that contained the following ingredients.

Makes: *2 portions*

3.5 oz.	Potatoes	1/4 cup	Vegetable oil
6 oz.	Carrots	2.5 oz.	Dairy blend
4 oz.	Tomato sauce	1 cup	Biscuit mix
4 oz.	Chopped celery	5 oz.	Plain beans
1/4 tsp.	Salt	1 1/3 tbsp.	Chili powder
4 oz.	Poultry or ground beef		

From time to time, broccoli or another nutritious vegetable would be substituted in place of carrots.

TAKEN FROM: John Diedrich, "Sheriff's Office Sour on Jail Nutraloaf Settlement," *Milwaukee-Wisconsin Journal Sentinel*, January 14, 2013.

tions on food, taking away food has always been sort of legally right on the line," says David Fathi, director of the National Prison Project for the American Civil Liberties Union [ACLU].

There's no guidance from the government on using the loaf, but the American Correctional Association, which accredits prisons and sets best practices for the industry, discourages using food as a disciplinary measure.

The Federal Bureau of Prisons says it has never used the loaf in its facilities. Still, the loaf persists in other parts of the corrections system, and no agencies or organizations are keeping track of where and how often it's used.

So Benson Li, the former president of the Association of Correctional Food Service Affiliates and the food service director at the Los Angeles County jail, offered to help us find that out.

At a recent meeting of the association, Li conducted an informal survey at the request of NPR. About 40 percent of the prisons and jails that responded said their use of the loaf is diminishing, 30 percent said they do not use nutraloaf, and about 20 percent said their use was about the same or slightly growing.

Li says that, overall, the results suggest that the loaf is gradually being phased out.

"[Prisons and jails] are using less or some of them are using sparingly—maybe just two to three times in the last year," he says.

Li says he thinks one of the reasons for this is that prisoners have been challenging the loaf in the courts.

"You have seen a lot of different inmate claims and lawsuits against the Eighth Amendment in different states," he says.

One of the provisions of the Eighth Amendment is that "cruel and unusual punishment" not be inflicted on prisoners. So the prisoners who are filing these suits are hoping the courts will rule that chewing on loaf day after day is unconstitutional. And, believe it or not, there is precedent: In the 1970s, the Supreme Court ruled that a potato-y prison paste called grue should be outlawed under the Eighth Amendment.

The loaf has held up better than grue. Of the 22 cases brought since the beginning of 2012 alone, none has succeeded. But Li's informal survey suggests that the court cases are making the corrections industry increasingly squeamish about serving it.

And Fathi of the ACLU says this is part of a bigger transformation happening in the industry.

"The fading of the use of nutraloaf is part of a larger long-term trend toward professionalization and, in most respects, more humane conditions of confinement," he says.

> *"While it would be virtually impossible to statistically isolate disenfranchisement from the myriad other risk factors that disproportionately affect that population ... history has shown that human rights violations almost always lead to adverse health outcomes."*

Prisoner Disenfranchisement Is Wrong and Dangerous

Jonathan Purtle

In the following viewpoint, Jonathan Purtle argues against the concept of felon disenfranchisement, maintaining that the practice unfairly robs individuals convicted of felonies of their political voice. Further, he asserts that this form of disenfranchisement has a detrimental effect on the health of underrepresented groups. In particular, Purtle says that such policies are especially disadvantageous to African Americans. Purtle is an assistant professor in health management and policy at Drexel University and the cofounder of the blog The Public's Health.

As you read, consider the following questions:

1. According to Purtle, how are felon disenfranchisement laws similar to Jim Crow laws, and how do they differ?

2. According to Purtle, how has felon disenfranchisement affected the outcomes of important national elections?

3. According to Purtle, how has felon disenfranchisement potentially been detrimental to the health of African Americans?

Consider two things:

- Life expectancy at birth for an African American male born in Philadelphia is 7.6 years shorter than a white male (67.5 years vs. 75.1).

- About 13% of African American men in the United States are prohibited from voting compared to 2.5% of the general voting-age population.

Felon disenfranchisement policies are the reason for the latter. I set out to explore whether they might be a cause of the former in an article published in the *American Journal of Public Health.*

How Felon Disenfranchisement Works

Felon disenfranchisement policies prevent people convicted of felonies, which include both violent and nonviolent crimes, from voting while incarcerated, on probation, on parole, or even after they have completed their sentences; the specifics vary by state. These policies disproportionately impact African Americans—a situation that reflects the discriminatory origins from which the policies emerged. Felon disenfranchisement policies proliferated across the nation after 1870, when the 15th Amendment gave African Americans the right to vote, forcing white land owners to find a new mechanism to uphold power structures. But unlike other Jim Crow–era barriers to the ballot box, such as literacy tests and poll taxes, felon disenfranchisement policies have withstood the test of time.

About 7.7% of voting-age African Americans are currently prohibited from voting compared to 2.5% of the U.S. population. Pennsylvania is among the more progressive states in this regard; only current prisoners are prevented from casting ballots, with 2.5% of the state's African Americans (0.6% of all races) disenfranchised, according to the Sentencing Project. New Jersey prohibits people from voting while in prison, on parole or probation, disenfranchising 5.5% of its African American residents (1.5% of all races). When the analysis is limited to males, who are far more likely to be imprisoned, it finds that 13% of African American men are disenfranchised nationwide. An African American male born today has a 1-in-3 chance of being disenfranchised at some point in his life.

If a group of people can't vote, the politicians who care about their health needs might be less likely to win elections.

Sociologists Christopher Uggen and Jeff Manza, who wrote the book of felon disenfranchisement [*Locked Out: Felon Disenfranchisement and American Democracy*], estimated the extent to which these policies impacted election outcomes between 1978 and 2000. The researchers gathered data on voter turnout, party preference, and rates of disenfranchisement to explore whether U.S. Senate and presidential election outcomes would have been different if the incarcerated population had been able to vote. Assuming that 70% of prisoners would have voted for Democrats and that 35% would have voted in presidential elections and 24% in Senate elections, all based on voting patterns of similar populations outside, they found that:

- Seven U.S. Senate elections won by Republicans would have been won by Democrats;

- Democrats would have maintained control of the U.S. Senate between 1986 and 2002; and that

- Al Gore would have defeated George W. Bush in Florida by more than 80,000 votes in the 2000 presidential election.

121

In another study, Manza and Uggen looked at how U.S. election outcomes would have been different if disenfranchised people on probation and parole—not those currently in prison—were able to vote (a policy that two-thirds of Americans support) and found that five Senate elections won by Republicans would have been won by Democrats. Lastly, they assessed how election outcomes would have been different if former prisoners who had completed their sentences were able to vote (a policy that 80 percent of Americans support) and found that three Senate elections won by Republicans would have been won by Democrats, and that Gore *still* would have defeated Bush in Florida and won the presidency.

The Effects of Felon Disenfranchisement

Felon disenfranchisement policies skew election outcomes in favor of the Republican Party. But are Republicans in Congress in part to blame for racial health disparities? It's impossible to say for sure, but Democrats generally support more progressive policies that promote social equity and have the potential to reduce racial disparities in health.

A review of how members of Congress voted on key public health legislation in 2013 reveals that Republicans more frequently opposed bills with the potential to reduce disparities such as gun safety legislation (the firearm homicide rate among African American males ages 15–30 is 10 times higher than among their white counterparts, according to data from the Centers for Disease Control and Prevention) and supported bills that could further perpetuate disparities (such as cutting funding for nutrition assistance programs, like food stamps).

The [Patient Protection and] Affordable Care Act [also known as Obamacare] provides another example. The health insurance reform law will likely reduce racial disparities in health insurance (33% of African Americans were uninsured

The Racist Origins of Felon Disenfranchisement

The state laws that barred nearly six million people with felony convictions from voting in the midterm elections this month [November 2014] date from the late 19th and early 20th centuries, when Southern lawmakers were working feverishly to neutralize the black electorate.

Poll taxes, literacy tests, grandfather clauses and cross burnings were effective weapons in this campaign. But statutes that allowed correctional systems to arbitrarily and permanently strip large numbers of people of the right to vote were a particularly potent tool in the campaign to undercut African American political power.

This racially freighted system has normalized disenfranchisement in the United States—at a time when our peers in the democratic world rightly see it as an aberration. It has also stripped one in every 13 black persons of the right to vote—a rate four times that of nonblacks nationally. At the same time, it has allowed disenfranchisement to move beyond that black population—which makes up 38 percent of those denied the vote—into the body politic as a whole. One lesson here is that punishments designed for one pariah group can be easily expanded to include others as well.

Brent Staples, "The Racist Origins of Felon Disenfranchisement," New York Times, *November 18, 2014.*

at some point during 2005 compared to 20% of whites), eventually resulting in reductions in disparities in access to health care and ultimately decreasing, to some extent, disparities in health outcomes. The GOP has gone to great lengths to try and "repeal Obamacare."

The right to "universal and equal suffrage" is clearly printed on the Universal Declaration of Human Rights. U.S. Attorney General Eric Holder has called on states across the nation to repeal felon disenfranchisement policies. Public health researchers should do the same. While it would be virtually impossible to statistically isolate disenfranchisement from the myriad other risk factors that disproportionately affect that population (e.g., poverty, unemployment, trauma) and prove that the policies negatively impact health, history has shown that human rights violations almost always lead to adverse health outcomes.

"*The proposal to automatically restore felons' right to vote as soon as they have completed their sentences is short-sighted and bad public policy.*"

Prisoner Disenfranchisement Should Not Be Abandoned

Hans A. von Spakovsky

In the following viewpoint, Hans A. von Spakovsky argues in support of felon disenfranchisement laws. He contends that such laws are entirely constitutional and are, in fact, a necessary part of any successful democratic political system. As such, he says that these laws, no matter how unfair they may seem on the surface, should be kept intact. Von Spakovsky is a senior legal fellow with the Heritage Foundation and the coauthor of Who's Counting?: How Fraudsters and Bureaucrats Put Your Vote at Risk.

As you read, consider the following questions:

1. According to von Spakovsky, why is Florida's felon voting policy a good approach to re-enfranchising felons?

2. What problem does von Spakovsky see with anti-disenfranchisement advocates' position on felon voting policies?

Hans A. von Spakovsky, "Ex-Cons Should Prove They Deserve the Right to Vote," Heritage Foundation, 2013. Copyright © 2013 The Heritage Foundation. All rights reserved. Reproduced with permission.

3. How do felon voting policies give convicts an incentive to reform, according to von Spakovsky?

The proposal to automatically restore felons' right to vote as soon as they have completed their sentences is short-sighted and bad public policy. When presented as a measure of compassion and justice, it is also hypocritical, as automatic restoration is not in the best interests of felons or the general public.

Why Felon Disenfranchisement Works

Under Florida's current system, nonviolent offenders face a five-year waiting period—and violent felons must wait seven years—before their rights can be fully restored. The waiting period gives the Governor's Office of Executive Clemency the opportunity to review each felon's behavior since release to determine whether he has realized the seriousness of his past misbehavior and changed his ways.

It takes time to establish a track record. Yet it is the only method to find out if the felon is now participating in the social compact that governs our country and complying with the rules of a civil society.

An April 2012 report from the Florida Department of Corrections showed that the recidivism rate of felons ranged from 31 percent to 34 percent on average over a five-year period. Recidivism among those convicted of robbery, burglary and sex offenses reached or exceeded 50 percent, while the overall recidivism rate for felons committing nonviolent offenses also approached 50 percent.

Given that such a large number of felons are rearrested and re-incarcerated within a short time after their release, Florida's waiting period is a perfectly reasonable requirement.

Where the Advocates Are Wrong

Advocates of automatic restoration also seem reluctant to mention that voting rights aren't the only rights people lose

Felon Disenfranchisement

We believe that applying Section 2 of the Voting Rights Act to felon disenfranchisement provisions raises grave constitutional concerns. Chiefly, the plaintiffs' interpretation calls for a reading of the statute which would prohibit a practice that the Fourteenth Amendment permits Florida to maintain. As a matter of statutory construction, we should avoid such an interpretation. The case for rejecting the plaintiffs' reading of the statute is particularly strong here, where Congress has expressed its intent to exclude felon disenfranchisement provisions from Voting Rights Act scrutiny. Accordingly, we affirm the district court's grant of summary judgment to the defendants on the Voting Rights Act claim. . . .

Indeed, throughout history, criminal disenfranchisement provisions have existed as a punitive device. When the Fourteenth Amendment was ratified, twenty-nine of thirty-six states had some form of criminal disenfranchisement law.

Today, forty-eight states have some form of criminal disenfranchisement provision. Although Florida's felon disenfranchisement law may be among the most restrictive, Florida hardly stands alone in its long-standing use of these laws.

Johnson v. Governor of the State of Florida,
United States Court of Appeals, Eleventh Circuit, April 12, 2005.

when convicted of a felony. In Florida, as in most states, they also lose their right to own a gun, hold public office, sit on a jury, and obtain certain types of professional and occupational licenses. Many such rights can never be restored without a full pardon.

Why are advocates of felon voting rights silent on this count? If they believe felons deserve automatic restoration of the right to vote because they have paid their debt to society, shouldn't all rights be restored?

If they believe restoring voting rights will help "reintegrate" felons into civil society, why don't they push for automatic restoration of all other rights, including the fundamental rights to serve on a jury, work as a police officer, or own and carry a gun?

How can they be certain that a convicted drug dealer will exercise his right to vote in a responsible and trustworthy manner, yet not trust him to exercise his Second Amendment right responsibly? If a convicted burglar will vote as conscientiously as law-abiding citizens in close, local elections, why not trust her to make the right choices sitting on a jury or working as a police officer?

These omissions are a glaring inconsistency. Are advocates only interested in restoring the right to vote because they believe that will benefit them politically or ideologically in election contests?

A Better Approach

Several years ago, liberal groups unsuccessfully sued Florida, claiming that the state's rules were unconstitutional and a violation of the Voting Rights Act. In *Johnson v. [Governor of the State of Florida]*, a federal appeals court dismissed those claims, noting that "criminal disenfranchisement provisions have existed as a punitive device" throughout history.

People truly concerned with the well-being of felons and their successful reintegration into civil society would want the type of system Florida has. Felons have, by definition, knowingly and intentionally violated the laws of society. A five- or seven-year waiting period gives felons the opportunity—and an incentive—to prove they are deserving of exercising their right to vote.

Such an incentive can only encourage their rehabilitation—it should not be a "freebie," restored automatically as though it has no value at all.

Periodical and Internet Sources Bibliography

The following articles have been selected to supplement the diverse views presented in this chapter.

Keri Blakinger	"Solitary Confinement Is State-Sanctioned Torture, and It's Putting Everyone at Risk," *Quartz*, February 26, 2015.
Jamelle Bouie	"The Jim Crow Zombie That Won't Die," Daily Beast, February 11, 2014.
Roger Clegg	"Felons and the Vote," Center for Equal Opportunity, March 30, 2015.
Adam Cohen	"Can Food Be Cruel and Unusual Punishment?," *Time*, April 2, 2012.
Joseph A. Fiorenza and Neil F. Blumofe	"Commentary: Solitary Confinement Reform Is Necessary," *Houston Chronicle*, April 15, 2015.
Donn Rowe	"Why We Need 'Solitary,'" *New York Post*, December 10, 2012.
Hans A. von Spakovsky and Roger Clegg	"Felon Voting and Unconstitutional Congressional Overreach," Heritage Foundation, February 11, 2015.
Alexander J. Spanos	"The Eighth Amendment and Nutraloaf: A Recipe for Disaster," *Journal of Contemporary Health Law and Policy*, vol. 30, no. 1, Fall 2013.
Roy Speckhardt	"Felons Deserve the Right to Vote," *Huffington Post*, August 7, 2013.
Brent Staples	"The Racist Origins of Felon Disenfranchisement," *New York Times*, November 18, 2014.
Daniel Weeks	"Should Felons Lose the Right to Vote?," *Atlantic*, January 7, 2014.

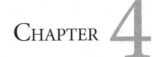

Do Prison Alternatives Work?

Chapter Preface

As America's prisons have become increasingly over-crowded, criminal justice experts have looked for ways to punish and rehabilitate offenders without resorting to incarceration. Over the years, numerous prison alternatives have been developed and used, but few have been as broadly embraced as probation. A unique sentencing option that affords offenders the opportunity to avoid prison time by agreeing to follow certain court-imposed conditions, probation has been a valuable tool in the struggle to control the exploding prison population and keep nonviolent, low-level offenders in their communities.

The concept of probation was first introduced in the American criminal justice system in Boston, Massachusetts, in 1841. That year, boot maker and criminal justice reform advocate John Augustus began providing bail for first-time offenders who wanted to get out of prison and achieve real reform. By helping those he freed to overcome the personal issues that landed them behind bars in the first place and guiding them back to being productive members of society, Augustus proved that probation could work as a viable alternative to incarceration. In 1878, Massachusetts recognized Augustus's success by enacting the nation's first probation law. Although similar legislation quickly followed in other states, it wasn't until the passage of the Probation Act of 1925 that probation was formally adopted as an official sentencing option in federal court. Since that time, probation has become a standard sanction across the country.

In the modern criminal justice system, probation is a two-step process. The first step is a presentence investigation that begins when an offender admits to or is found guilty of committing a crime. When this happens, the court assigns a probation officer to conduct an investigation into the offender's personal and criminal background and deliver a detailed report that the presiding judge will use to determine whether or not the individual in question qualifies for a probation sentence. If the judge decides to put the individual on probation, the second part of the process, supervision of the offender, begins. For the duration of his or her time on probation, the offender is monitored and assisted by an appointed probation officer who ensures that the offender adheres to the specific conditions of his or her sentence. Often these conditions require offenders to complete activities such as attending rehabilitation or place restrictions on travel or things that the offender can do. If the offender violates the terms of his or her probation, he or she may face additional sanctions or even incarceration.

Since it was first adopted, probation has garnered a considerable amount of both praise and criticism. Advocates of probation point to the obvious fact that it keeps people out of prison and potentially gives them a better shot at achieving full rehabilitation. They also typically cite the fact that by keeping people out of prison, probation saves taxpayers on the enormous cost involved in incarcerating criminal offenders. On the other hand, critics of probation argue that it is not always an effective means of achieving reform because it makes it too easy for offenders to continue their illicit activities. Some also contend that probation conditions are often overly oppressive and unfairly enforced.

The ongoing debate over probation has led corrections experts to develop a number of other approaches to sentencing options that may offer a better solution to America's prisons.

The following chapter examines drug courts, electronic monitoring, and public shaming as alternatives to incarceration. The authors debate the effectiveness of these alternatives and whether these options can have a significant impact on solving America's prison problems.

> "Drug courts may actually increase the
> criminal justice involvement of people
> charged with drug law violations and
> people with drug problems."

Drug Courts Are Not a Good Alternative for Drug Offenders

Margaret Dooley-Sammuli and Nastassia Walsh

In the following viewpoint, Margaret Dooley-Sammuli and Nas-
tassia Walsh argue that the use of drug courts as an alternative
to traditional trials and prison sentences has generally failed to
help people with drug problems. They contend that rather than
keeping nonviolent drug offenders out of prison, drug courts are
actually leading to a higher rate of incarceration among people
struggling with substance abuse issues. Dooley-Sammuli is an
American Civil Liberties Union (ACLU) policy director, and
Walsh is the program manager of county solutions and innova-
tion at the National Association of Counties in Washington, DC.

As you read, consider the following questions:

1. According to the authors, how do drug courts increase
   the criminal justice involvement of people with drug
   problems?

2. What observations do the authors make about the effectiveness of drug treatment programs that people are required to attend through drug courts?

3. According to the authors, what would make drug courts more effective?

D rug addiction is a health problem. So why are U.S. drug policies still seeking solutions within the criminal justice system?

The use of drug courts—programs that seek to reduce drug use through mandated drug treatment and close judicial oversight—has grown drastically over the last 20 years thanks to moving success stories and enthusiastic proponents within the criminal justice system. In Maryland, the Drug Treatment Court Commission was established in 1993, and Baltimore city's first drug treatment court started in 1994. There are now 39 treatment courts in the state. These success stories are real and deserve to be celebrated, but they provide only a partial picture.

The Problem with Drug Courts

On the face of it, drug courts appear to be aligned with a growing sentiment that incarceration is not an effective response to drug use and that treatment is a better option because it gets at the root of the problem. In other words, drug courts are promoted as more like a public health approach. Unfortunately, drug courts appear to be a case of good intentions being mistaken for a real solution.

Drug courts may actually increase the criminal justice involvement of people charged with drug law violations and people with drug problems. In a Baltimore drug court, for example, research has found that participants were incarcerated more often while in drug court and for the same amount of total days compared with a control group of probationers,

Drug Courts Are Not the Answer

There is no doubt that drug courts—programs that seek to reduce drug use through mandated treatment and close judicial oversight—were created and continue to be run with unflagging dedication and concern for the health and well-being of individuals and communities. Nor is there any doubt that drug court judges and their staffs have helped change, even save, many lives. Most drug court judges have felt deep satisfaction in being able to help participants overcome chaos, illness and despair. There is, indeed, no shortage of success stories. Many participants have had dramatic, life-altering experiences in drug courts. Criminal justice sanctions do indeed deter some people from using drugs, and some people will stop their drug use when faced with the threat of such sanctions. These observations, however, do not end the discussion.

Most interventions help at least some people, and drug courts are no exception. But it is important to consider the full range of drug court impacts, both positive and negative, on all participants as well as on the criminal justice and other systems. It is also important to consider drug court outcomes within the larger context of potential policy options and practices to reduce drug arrests, incarceration and problematic drug use. In this light, the benefits of drug courts pale considerably.

"Drug Courts Are Not the Answer:
Toward a Health-Centered Approach to Drug Use,"
Drug Policy Alliance, March 22, 2011.

generally for program violations (not even including the incarceration later experienced by the 45 percent of people expelled from the program).

According to two new reports, "Addicted to Courts" and "Drug Courts Are Not the Answer," the research clearly shows that drug courts can come with significant unintended negative consequences that make these programs little, if any, better than the system they intend to improve upon. In fact, drug courts may actually be making the criminal justice system more punitive toward addiction because the participants most likely to do well in drug courts are those without a drug problem (about one-third of participants, according to one national survey).

Based on our analyses of the existing research, we have independently come to the same conclusion as several academics and even the federal government's [Government] Accountability Office: Claims that drug courts have significantly reduced costs, incarceration or drug use are unsupported by the evidence.

More troubling is that drug courts may actually increase the criminal justice involvement of people with drug problems. The widespread use of incarceration as a sanction in drug courts—for failing a drug test, missing an appointment or having a hard time following the strict rules of the court—means that some participants end up serving more time behind bars than if they had not entered drug court. And some participants may face longer sentences when they are ejected from drug court than those who did not enter drug court in the first place (often because they lost the opportunity to plead to a lesser charge). Even people who are not in drug court may be negatively affected by them, since drug courts have been associated with increased arrests and incarceration in some cases. This is often because law enforcement and others believe people will "get help" if they are arrested. But drug courts have limited capacity and strict eligibility requirements, which mean that many of the people arrested end up conventionally sentenced instead.

A Troubling Outlook

Some might argue that, for the right results, increased criminal justice involvement is worth it. But it isn't. Treatment through the criminal justice system, including drug courts, is not found to be more effective than treatment in the community—though it is significantly more expensive. A federal study by the Substance Abuse and Mental Health Services Administration, for example, showed that people referred to treatment from the criminal justice system do not fare better than those referred through other means (such as a loved one or an employer). And, according to the Washington State Institute for Public Policy, drug courts do not reduce recidivism by even half a percentage point more than treatment in the community without a judge's oversight.

More than 1.4 million people are arrested every year in this country simply for possessing a small amount of drugs for personal use—about half for marijuana. Only some of them have a drug problem and need treatment. Even if drug courts were greatly expanded to cover all of the people in the justice system who needed treatment, between 500,000 and 1 million people would still be ejected from a drug court and sentenced conventionally every year. Drug courts would be more appropriate and certainly produce better results (at least in terms of cost savings) if they focused on people with drug addiction who are facing prison time for more serious offenses.

> *"Given the success of drug courts, and the projected savings if more programs were implemented, the United States should use drug courts to save taxpayers money and effectively treat criminals with drug problems."*

Drug Courts Are a Good Alternative for Drug Offenders

Jessica Huseman

In the following viewpoint, Jessica Huseman argues that drug courts are an effective and efficient alternative to incarceration for criminal offenders with drug problems. Citing the economic and practical benefits of drug courts, she also goes on to suggest that more such courts should be established nationally. Huseman is a journalism student and a contributing writer for the Hechinger Report *as well as a former intern at the National Center for Policy Analysis.*

As you read, consider the following questions:

1. According to Huseman, why is probation an ineffective alternative to incarceration?

2. According to Husemen, how do drug courts benefit families?

3. Why does Huseman believe that more drug courts should be established?

Drug courts are judicially supervised programs that provide long-term treatment and other services to nonviolent drug law offenders. Cases can be referred to drug courts in lieu of or in addition to traditional criminal punishment, such as incarceration or probation.

For a period lasting a minimum of one year, offenders receive treatment and help readjusting to life outside of prison and without drug use. Participants are randomly drug tested and regularly appear before a judge to review their progress. They can be sanctioned or rewarded based on such behavioral criteria as attending meetings, staying drug free and working.

Drug courts are a relatively recent phenomenon. The number of drug courts has increased from zero in 1988 to more than 2,000 in 2008. The federal government is a major funder of the courts, spending $40 million on them in fiscal year 2009. Many say that drug courts save taxpayers money and are more effective than prison alone. But is that true?

The Benefits of Drug Courts

The High Cost of Imprisonment. After almost three decades of growth, the U.S. prison population reached 2.3 million in 2007. This large prison population comes with a hefty price tag. In 2007, the United States spent $44 billion on the prison system—four times (or $33 billion) more than in 1987. The average annual cost of incarceration is $24,000 per inmate. A number of states spend as much or more money on their corrections system as they do on higher education, including Connecticut, Vermont, Delaware, Oregon and Michigan.

The Rate of Drug Use Among Criminals. More than 60 percent of those arrested test positive for alcohol or some type of drug. Some 80 percent of convicted criminals abuse drugs or alcohol, and more than 50 percent can be defined as clinically addicted. Prison itself does little to curb drug abuse:

- In 2004, about 21 percent of prisoners were in jail for a drug-related offense—this percentage has not changed since 1994.

- More than half of inmates will return to prison within three years of their release.

- Even if they do not return to prison, 95 percent of convicts will return to drug use.

Similarly, probation, which is often considered an alternative to incarceration, is not an effective deterrent to drug use. Between 50 percent and 70 percent of probationers fail to comply with drug testing and treatment requirements, which only subjects them to more jail time at taxpayer expense.

The Effectiveness of Drug Courts. Professors at the University of Pennsylvania found that drug courts had a compliance rate six times higher than any other current method of treating criminals with drug addictions. They also found that drug courts were two to three times more successful than other methods in reducing recidivism, drug use and unemployment.

Studies have also shown that drug users who have children are more likely to complete a drug court program than any other type of treatment. Among families whose children have been taken away because of their parents' drug use, reunification rates are 50 percent higher if a parent completes a drug court program, and those children spend less time, on average, in out-of-home placements.

Drug Courts Save Money. According to the National Association of Drug Court Professionals, cost savings due to drug courts range from $4,000 to more than $12,000 per client. Nationwide, for every dollar invested in drug courts, taxpayers save as much as $3.36 in avoided criminal justice costs alone.

Recidivism

Graduates of drug courts are, according to current evaluations, less likely to be rearrested than persons processed through traditional court mechanics. Findings from drug court evaluations show that participation in drug courts results in fewer rearrests and reconvictions, or longer periods between arrests.

- An analysis of research findings from 76 drug courts found a 10% reduction in rearrest. . . .

- An analysis of 30 drug court evaluations found an average 13% decline in the rate of reconvictions for a new offense.

- A meta-analysis of 57 studies estimated that participation in a drug court program would produce an 8% decline in crime relative to no treatment.

- A Government Accountability Office report found that 13 of 17 courts reporting on post-program recidivism measured reductions between 4 and 25 percentage points in rearrests and reconvictions.

- An evaluation of drug courts in Florida and Missouri . . . found a substantially lower rearrest rate for drug court graduates relative to the comparison group. . . .

- Six drug courts in New York State averaged a 29% reduction in rearrest measured over 3 years following participants' initial arrest. . . .

- An evaluation of the Multnomah County, Oregon, drug court found a 24% reduction in drug arrests for participants thirteen years after initial entry into the program.

Ryan S. King and Jill Pasquarella, "Drug Courts: A Review of the Evidence," The Sentencing Project, April 2009.

A 30-month U.S. Department of Justice study of Portland, Oregon's Multnomah County drug court, the second oldest in the nation, found that it saved almost $5,000 per participant, on average, totaling more than $1.5 million per year. The net savings included the actual cost of judges, courtrooms and drug tests, avoided trials and jail time, and avoided victimization costs, such as lost workdays, medical expenses and so forth.

Managing an offender through drug court costs more than probation alone, but much less than jail or prison. According to a statewide evaluation of drug court programs in Kentucky:

- In 2004, it cost an average of $1,256 per year for an offender on traditional probation.

- It cost $3,083 to manage an offender through drug court, including administrative and treatment costs.

- By contrast, the one-year cost of maintaining an offender in jail was $9,676 or $17,194 in prison.

The Need for More Drug Courts. The U.S. Department of Justice recently identified 1.2 million people in the criminal justice system who would be eligible for drug court but do not have access due to their location.

According to estimates from the National Association of Drug Court Professionals:

- Drug court programs only serve about half of those who qualify, and less than 10 percent of those arrestees at risk for drug and alcohol abuse who would benefit.

- If the programs treated all currently eligible individuals, it would save $2.14 for every $1 invested, totaling $1.17 billion annually.

- Furthermore, if drug courts were expanded to treat all arrestees at risk for drug or alcohol abuse or dependence, it would save an estimated $3.36 for every $1 invested, totaling an additional $32.3 billion annually.

143

Given the success of drug courts, and the projected savings if more programs were implemented, the United States should use drug courts to save taxpayers money and effectively treat criminals with drug problems.

> "*Prison is horrible. It's grossly inhumane. It's a huge waste of money. And there may finally be a way to (mostly) get rid of it.*"

Electronic Monitoring Is an Effective Alternative to Incarceration

Dylan Matthews

In the following viewpoint, Dylan Matthews argues in support of electronic monitoring as an alternative to incarceration. Noting that global positioning system (GPS) technology has made electronic monitoring far more effective and reliable than ever before, he contends that such devices are a perfect means of administering justice without unnecessarily exposing people to the dangers of incarceration and further increasing the already swollen populations of America's prisons. Matthews is a reporter who writes for Vox *and other online and print publications.*

As you read, consider the following questions:

1. According to Matthews, why does GPS technology make electronic monitoring more effective?

2. According to Matthews, why does GPS-enforced electronic monitoring need to be combined with an adequate system of punishment?

3. What is Matthews's solution to the problem of mass incarceration?

Prison is horrible. It's grossly inhumane. It's a huge waste of money. And there may finally be a way to (mostly) get rid of it.

In any given year, 3.2 percent of those in jail, 4.0 percent of state and federal prisoners, and 9.5 percent of juvenile detainees report having been sexually abused. A 2005 study found that the rate of physical assault was over 18 times higher for male inmates and 27 times higher for females relative to the general population.

The system that sends people to these inhumane pens where they're likely to get beaten and raped is baldly racist. For the same crimes, black men are typically sentenced to 20 percent longer stays than white men.

And taxpayers are paying through the nose for all this. About 2.2 million were incarcerated in 2012, accounting for one in every 108 adults, a figure that has more than quadrupled since 1980, leading state spending on incarceration to rise nearly as fast. America imprisons more people than any other country, and has the highest incarceration rate. And this wrecks communities. Mass incarceration weakens the economy and increases teen pregnancy in areas where many residents are sent away, and harms the children of the incarcerated in ways that persist for decades, among many other damaging effects.

So why do prisons exist? In theory, because we need them. They keep bad guys off the street. They give people a reason to not commit crimes. They provide a place where violent or otherwise threatening people can be rehabilitated.

But prisons aren't the only way to accomplish those goals. Technological advancements are, some observers say, making it possible to replace the current system of large-scale imprisonment, in large part, with alternatives that are not as expensive, inhumane, or socially destructive, and which at the same time do a better job of controlling crime. The most promising of these alternatives fits on an ankle.

Why GPS Changes Things

While the idea of house arrest has been around for millennia, it has always suffered from one key defect as a crime control tool: you can escape. Sure, you could place guards on the homes where prisoners are staying, but it's much easier to secure a prison with a large guard staff than it is a thousand different houses with a guard or two apiece.

Today, we have something better than guards: satellites. The advent of GPS [global positioning system] location tracking means it's now possible for authorities to be alerted the second a confinee leaves their home. That not just enables swift response in the event of escape; it deters escape by making clear to detainees that they won't get away with it.

Researchers have tested electronic monitoring as an alternative approach to parole, probation, or other criminal punishments that fall short of imprisonment—and it's been a huge success. An Urban Institute analysis found that electronic monitoring reduces the odds of rearrest by 23.5 percent relative to traditional probation, and a randomized study in Switzerland found major advantages to electronic monitoring compared to mandated community service. Results from a Swedish trial in which prisoners were offered early release under electronic monitoring were similarly promising. The threat of electronically enforced house arrest appears to provide a strong deterrent effect; when Santa Fe County, New Mexico, started threatening drunk drivers with home confinement if they failed to install ignition interlocks (which prevent a car from starting until the driver passes a breathalyzer test), installation rates skyrocketed.

The most intriguing evidence comes from Argentina, where Harvard's Rafael Di Tella and Torcuato Di Tella University's Ernesto Schargrodsky found that electronic monitoring cuts recidivism nearly in half relative to a prison sentence. That raises the possibility that electronic monitoring could be more than merely a supplement to prisons. It could replace many of them. The program evaluated used something a bit less technologically sophisticated than GPS tracking. Offenders wore an ankle bracelet that transmitted a signal to a receptor in their home. If the signal is interrupted, or the device appears to be manipulated, or the vital signs of the individual are not being transmitted from the bracelet, then the receptor calls it in.

Di Tella and Schargrodsky's evidence is particularly compelling because the decision of whether to give Argentinian arrestees house arrest or prison was made randomly. In most countries, electronic monitoring is offered to defendants judged to be less dangerous, so you'd expect those sentenced to it to re-offend less than those sent to prison. "If you show someone released into monitoring has lower recidivism, all you show is that the judge was successful and identified the person who was less dangerous," Di Tella notes.

But in Argentina, judges are randomly assigned to cases, and strict and lenient judges differ wildly in their inclination to use electronic monitoring. The result was that extremely high-risk people were sometimes given electronic monitoring and extremely low-risk people were sometimes thrown into jail—it was just random. The leniency of some judges meant that there were "people accused for the second time of murder [who] were still given electronic monitoring," Di Tella says. Di Tella and Schargrodsky had stumbled upon a true, randomized experiment, and the result was being monitored instead of imprisoned caused people to re-offend less.

Who Do We Actually Imprison?

So, if electronic monitoring can work just as well as prison—and keeps prisoners from being physically and sexually assaulted by guards and other inmates, and saves money, and perhaps even allows some inmates to earn a living while serving time—why not switch?

Di Tella says he isn't ready to make that dramatic a shift. For one thing, GPS probably isn't prepared to deal with genuinely violent and dangerous offenders just yet. In one case, a GPS assignee named Angel Fernandez escaped and proceeded to murder a family of four, including children aged 8 and 10; the ensuing backlash was enough to end the program in Argentina. Similar incidents have occurred in the UK [United Kingdom], which has seen the use of GPS tagging increase considerably in recent years.

But the fact of the matter is that rapists and murderers are a distinct minority of the prison population, at least in the United States. According to the Bureau of Justice Statistics as of 2011 only 12.6 percent of state prisoners in 2011 were there for murder, 1.5 percent for negligent manslaughter, and 12.4 percent for rape or sexual assault. That's only 26.5 percent of the overall prison population. The numbers are even starker in federal prisons: only 3.8 percent of prisoners committed any kind of violent crime.

If you look at who's being sent to prison in a given year, the share is smaller still. In 2011, only 2 percent were admitted for murder, 0.7 percent for negligent manslaughter, and 5.4 percent for rape or sexual assault. Because they face long sentences, people convicted of homicide and rape make up a considerably larger share of a prison's population than they do of a given year's admissions. But that means that in a typical year, 91.9 percent of the people who are thrown into prison are there for something else. The vast majority of the people getting locked up aren't killers or rapists.

Which isn't to say they're angels, either. 26.9 percent of state prisoners are there for robbery, assault, or another violent offense; 18.7 percent are there on non-robbery property crime charges; 16.6 percent on drug charges; and 10.6 percent on public order charges (which includes everything from weapons charges to drunk driving to contempt of court to prostitution). Even if you support legalizing drugs and sex work, you probably want the government to do something about people who rob or assault each other. The question is whether that "something" has to be prison.

Making Punishment Predictable

Better technology only strengthens the case. Previous electronic monitoring systems, like the one Di Tella and Schargrodsky studied, involving bracelets transmitting signals to a receptor, fell short in cases of escape. They left police with no sense of where escapees have gone. GPS tagging changes that (at least for confinees who flee with their bracelet still on). "The GPS tagging technology now available enables the development of a tagging regime that works," Rory Geoghegan, a crime policy researcher at the British think tank Policy Exchange, writes, "One that protects and controls offenders, but also aids them to change, because constant supervision of a wearer's location accords with the academic evidence that certainty and swiftness of sanctions is more critical than the severity of any sanction ultimately invoked, and is therefore the best basis for behavior change."

The latter point is crucial. While better technology is making replacing prison with GPS-enforced house arrest possible, it needs to be combined with a system of punishment that guarantees a speedy reprimand if the rules are broken. If escapes aren't answered quickly, either with an immediate return to home confinement with increased supervision or with a return to prison, the system will fail. If people are punished when they have not in fact violated the rules, the system will fail. And if the costs of violating the rules are vague and un-certain—even if they're also quite severe—the system will fail.

This paradigm, pioneered by UCLA [University of California, Los Angeles] criminologist Mark Kleiman, has been gaining traction for years, and has shown great promise when applied to drug probation in Hawaii (and, later, Texas and Michigan), punishment for drunk driving in South Dakota and parole enforcement in Washington. There are two benefits to "swift and certain" sanctions. The first is that it *works*. The Hawaii system—which replaced an approach where drug probationers faced lengthy jail sentences for breaking probation, but where those sentences were rarely imposed, with one where regular drug tests were expected and missing or failing one guaranteed a night in jail—reduced recidivism by about 50 percent. The second is that it's way, way more humane. Throwing people in jail for five, ten, even twenty years for a drug violation is obscene. Swift and certain sanction not only reduces crime, it reduces punishment and makes it less horrible.

A Solution . . .

The US should:

1. Move those imprisoned for offenses short of homicide or sexual assault to GPS-supervised house arrest as soon as is practicable, with a guaranteed, immediate prison stay for those who violate its terms.

2. Reserve prisons for repeat offenders and those who've committed truly heinous crimes.

There are obviously other details to be worked out. You wouldn't want people convicted of domestic violence to be sentenced to home confinement with their victims, for instance; in those cases, some kind of alternate housing would have to be offered to ensure separation.

But if successful, this plan could reduce admissions by at least half, probably much more. Hopefully, this will just be a temporary measure. In principle, it could get to the point technologically where house arrest becomes as hard to escape as prison is. At that point, abolishing prison outright starts to become imaginable. UK home secretary David Blunkett spoke too soon when he referred to electronic monitoring as "prison without bars," but that dream is attainable. As Kleiman once put it, "My view is that if you know where someone is, you don't have to put them in the cage."

> *"Advocates of the [electronic monitoring] bracelet argue [that it] is cheaper than prison, ensures public safety, and allows the person on the monitor to go about their business. The problem is, like everything in criminal justice, electronic monitoring is not that simple."*

Electronic Monitoring Is Not an Effective Alternative to Incarceration

James Kilgore

In the following viewpoint, James Kilgore argues against the widespread use of electronic monitoring as an alternative to incarceration. He suggests that electronic monitoring, while technically efficient, is a pervasive violation of personal freedom that can all too easily be used in a discriminatory fashion. Kilgore, an author, activist, and former prison inmate, has written extensively on mass incarceration and the American prison system.

As you read, consider the following questions:

1. Why do people on electronic monitoring have less freedom than prisoners, according to Kilgore?

2. According to Kilgore, why is electronic monitoring a potential punishment for being poor?

3. How might electronic monitoring be used to promote racial profiling, according to Kilgore?

In a troubled criminal justice system desperately looking for alternatives to incarceration, electronic monitoring is trending. North Carolina has tripled the use of electronic monitors since 2011. California has placed 7,500 people on GPS [global positioning system] ankle bracelets as part of a realignment program aimed to reduce prison populations. SuperCom, an Israeli-based Smart ID and electronic monitor producer, announced in early July [2014] that they were jumping full force into the US market, predicting this will be a $6 billion a year global industry by 2018.

The praise singers of electronic monitoring are also resurfacing. Late last month, high-profile blogger Dylan Matthews posted a story on Vox, headlining "Prisons are terrible and there's finally a way to get rid of them." He enthusiastically argued that the most "promising" alternative "fits on an ankle." Joshua Earnest, press secretary for the [Barack] Obama White House, even suggested ankle bracelets as a solution to getting the 52,000 unaccompanied immigrant children out of border detention centers and military bases in the US Southwest.

The reasons behind this popular surge of monitoring are obvious: Prisons and jails (along with immigrant detention facilities) are overflowing from decades of mass incarceration. State, local and even federal authorities are looking for budget-cutting quick fixes. In the era of the smartphone, smart watch and smart textiles, nothing reads solution like technology.

On the surface, electronic monitoring (EM) seems like a simple alternative. Authorities put a bracelet on their charges, place a box in their house that receives a signal from the leg monitor and the parole, probation or ICE [US Immigration and Customs Enforcement] officer knows where the client is at all times. The advocates of the bracelet argue this is cheaper than prison, ensures public safety, and allows the person on the monitor to go about their business. The problem is, like everything in criminal justice, electronic monitoring is not that simple.

To begin with, even if you buy into the concept of electronic monitoring, the technology has lots of glitches. The most famous example was the October 2010 information overload that hit BI Incorporated, the nation's largest EM provider, cutting off data for 16,000 people on monitoring nationwide for 12 hours. Then there was the glitch in California in 2013 where hundreds of people with sex offense histories disappeared off the radar. Even more serious, though, are the false alarms. Journalist Mario Koran did an investigative report in Wisconsin in 2013 and found several instances where the devices had incorrectly reported that monitored people were not where they were supposed to be. In one case, a false report of Aaron Hicks being out of his house resulted in a 51-day jail sentence.

The Monitored: Fewer Rights than Prisoners

While the techno-geeks will likely address these glitches at some point, human rights questions and financial issues loom much larger. Surprisingly, those on monitors have fewer legal entitlements and rights than people in prison. While prisoners normally have entitlements such as the right to access legal materials along with daily quotas for caloric provision and exercise time, those on monitors have few, if any, such guarantees. The heart of the matter is that whether a person is on an ankle bracelet for parole, probation or pretrial release, the default position in most instances is house arrest.

In legalese, this is deprivation of liberty by technological means. To leave home, a person on a monitor needs permission for "movement" from their supervising officer and that permission has to be programmed into their device. More-over, parole or probation officers typically have the power to impose a "lockdown"—confining the person to their house 24 hours a day for any period without any judicial process. Fur-thermore, neither a decision to impose a lockdown nor deny movement offers channels of appeal for the monitored per-son.

My survey of the legislation in 12 states, with the largest number of people on GPS monitors for parole, reveals virtu-ally no legal rights or entitlements for those on a monitor. A sole exception is northwestern Ohio where a 50-page policy document guarantees a person two hours a week for grocery shopping and laundry, but warns that a request for such move-ment "will only be considered if no other person in the house-hold can provide this service." The document adds that the sole days of the year when the person may be permitted to at-tend family gatherings are Christmas and Thanksgiving for a maximum of two hours.

Interviews Truthout has conducted with people in four states who have been on monitors as a condition of parole or probation reveal that accessing movement remains an ongoing challenge. People complained of being unable to acquire per-mission to attend the funeral of a sibling, go to a job inter-view or visit a parent in the hospital. One interviewee in Illi-nois said, "There was literally a period of three straight months that I never left the house because of the hassle and bullshit of attempting to even get movement." Jean-Pierre Shackelford, who spent nearly three years on a monitor in Ohio, finally joined a church because it was one of the few activities for which he could get permission to leave the house. In a per-sonal interview, he referred to monitoring as "21st century slavery, electronic style."

Richard Stapleton, who worked for the Michigan Depart-ment of Corrections for over three decades, including several years on electronic monitoring policy, concurred with these criticisms. In a telephone conversation, he emphasized that the person on the monitor remained totally at the "whim of their [parole] agent." Rather than characterizing EM as an alternative, he referred to monitoring for people on parole as "another burdensome condition of extending . . . incarceration."

Who's Saving Money?

In addition to the crucial rights questions, the economics of EM don't add up: The monitors may save money for corrections departments and county sheriffs, but these costs frequently shift to the user or their family. A recent national survey of monitoring programs by National Public Radio [NPR] revealed that 49 states imposed daily fees for monitoring ranging from $5 to $25 a day. Given the escalating rates of criminal justice debt, which have been previously chronicled in Truthout, ankle bracelets run the risk of becoming yet another "alternative to incarceration" that ultimately leads people back behind bars for being poor.

The key corporate players in the electronic monitoring industry prompt further concern. BI, which controls about a third of the national market, is a totally owned subsidiary of notorious private prison operator the GEO Group, whose pro-incarceration lobbying and abuse of prisoners have been the focus of Truthout articles in the past. BI's contractual crown jewel is a five-year, $372 million pact to intensively supervise immigrants awaiting adjudication in asylum and deportation cases, including putting several thousand of them in ankle bracelets.

Joining BI as an EM market leader is private probation firm Sentinel Offender Services, the subject of a recent Human Rights Watch report that exposed the company's unethical actions and illicit profiteering in Southern states. Firms like the GEO Group and Sentinel are constantly looking for new clients, referred to as "net widening" in criminal justice

---

Alternatives to Incarceration

Like the plans of the early reformers, many current prison "reforms" share a common element: They perpetuate the fantasy that new forms of confinement, isolation, and surveillance will somehow set us all free.

At first glance, these alternatives may seem like a "win-win." Instead of taking place in a hellish institution, prison happens "in the comfort of your own home" (the ultimate American ad for anything). However, this change threatens to transform the very definition of "home" into one in which privacy, and possibly "comfort" as well, are subtracted from the equation. Perhaps the best example is the electronic monitor, an imprisonment device that is attached to the body at all times.

Maya Schenwar, "The Quiet Horrors of House Arrest,
Electronic Monitoring, and Other Alternative Forms
of Incarceration," Mother Jones, *January 22, 2015.*

---

circles. Perhaps BI already has their marketing eye fixed on those 52,000 immigrant children currently sitting in deportation limbo on our border.

People with Sex Offense Histories and Techno-Gentrification

However, nothing raises big-picture alarm bells like the EM regimes imposed on people with sex offense convictions. At least 11 states have legislation that damns people with certain categories of sex offenses to lifetime GPS. This techno-life-without-parole usually comes with exclusion zones. If the wearer comes within a specified distance (typically 1,000 to 2,000 feet) of a place where children congregate (schools, day care centers, parks) their ankle bracelet will sound an alarm.

Although there has been some backlash against such restrictions in Colorado, Kansas and a number of California cities, public sentiment against people with sex offenses remains vibrant.

The imposition of exclusion zones has implications beyond criminal justice. The recent report on criminalization of homelessness by the National Law Center on Homelessness and Poverty reveals a sharp escalation of laws against public sleeping, loitering, lying down in public, camping and begging. These laws are blunt instruments. Location monitoring offers the possibility of linking GPS to massive databases of undesirables, a virtual no-fly list for gentrified spaces. Indeed, those with histories of mental illness, violence, substance abuse, incarceration, unemployment, sex work, crossing gender barriers or even receiving state benefits could easily be included in online registries. Techno-racial profiling also lands on the possible agenda. Los Angeles has already applied electronic monitoring to people with histories of gang affiliation. With increasing numbers of people carrying GPS devices in their smartphones, developing urban population flow systems to keep the good people in and the bad people out becomes quite feasible. Each individual could end up with their own personalized techno-map of the city, indicating where they were and were not allowed.

While this may seem far-fetched, researchers at Deloitte University have taken it much further. In their 2013 scenario planning document, "Beyond the Bars," Alan Holden and Kara Shuler sketched a futuristic criminal justice monitoring system with a smart watch at the center that could allow two-way communication. The device could connect the user to a central database and a case manager. According to the authors, this system would use "advanced risk modeling, geospatial analytics, smartphone technology, and principles from the study of human behavior to achieve superior outcomes." These outcomes would ultimately be a more comprehensive system of controlling not only people's movement, but perhaps their biochemistry as well. In a *New York Times* piece, technology critic Evgeny Morozov called the vision of "Beyond the Bars": "the kind of cutting-edge innovation that only management consultants and tech entrepreneurs would be excited about." And perhaps private corrections executives who envision scoring the smart watch contracts.

British researcher Craig Patterson takes his critique of such techno-fixes to a higher level, arguing that the growth of EM has "been driven by a fascination with the potential of new technologies to deliver managerialist solutions to complex social problems and the broader processes of neoliberal globalization that have developed the markets in incarceration and social control." In other words, the use of futuristic technology becomes just another enactment of structural racism, and another method of criminalizing and policing poverty—rather than addressing its social roots.

Techno-Corrections: Spreading Like a Virus?

Over a decade ago, criminologist Tony Fabelo warned the audience at a meeting of the National Institute of Justice about what he called "techno-corrections." He maintained that techno-corrections had the potential to be useful, but added that "we must also anticipate the threats they pose to democracy . . . the infrastructure for increased intrusiveness by the state and its abusive control of both offenders and law-abiding citizens."

His final point was that "we need to start debating the ethical and legal questions that have to be answered if we are to understand how to prevent the state from using the techno-correctional establishment in ways inconsistent with constitutional or ethical standards." Unfortunately, little of that debate has taken place. Don't wait for the [Federal] Bureau of Prisons or the GEO Group to kick it off. We may witness angst over the [Edward] Snowden revelations or the spread of drones, but only a movement with a genuine alternative model for dealing with social problems stands a chance of derailing the techno-corrections train.

> "Even if it doesn't hurt one's reputation as much as a black mark on a background check, public humiliation forces a person to see and feel the consequences very, very personally."

Public Shaming Is a Good Substitute for Imprisonment

Brian Hampel

In the following viewpoint, Brian Hampel argues in support of using public shaming as an alternative to incarceration or other forms of punishment. In making his point, Hampel contends that public shaming sentences have a greater effect because they force criminals to confront their victims and come face-to-face with the consequences of their actions. At the time of writing, Hampel was a senior architecture student at Kansas State University.

As you read, consider the following questions:

1. According to Hampel, why is public shaming a stronger punishment for criminals than other punitive measures?

2. According to Hampel, why are attacks on personal reputation an effective deterrent?

3. According to Hampel, how is public shaming economically beneficial?

There has been a trend in the 21st century of unusual punishments for minor crimes, many of which involve some sort of humiliation or public shaming in lieu of more traditional jail sentences. Obviously, it never replaces prison sentences for the more dangerous and violent criminals who might need to be kept away from the general public, but misdemeanors around the country have been punished with deep embarrassment by creative judges with a flair for the dramatic. And it's great.

For example, Judge Peter Miller of Putnam County, Fla., has sentenced hundreds of shoplifters to stand outside the places they robbed with a huge sign that reads, "I stole from this store." In Nov. 2007, the *L.A. Times* reported on Judge Miller's methods alongside others in Ohio, Texas and San Francisco. It should not surprise one to learn that the sign method is not popular with the shoplifters being sentenced, but it might surprise one to learn that the sign method prevents a good deal of shoplifting.

The court doesn't keep statistics, but many Justice Department officials in Putnam County remark that they don't see many repeat offenders after the sign punishment. The embarrassment and guilt associated with the four-hour stints of carrying their signs are apparently enough to turn the offenders off of petty crime for a while, or at least to do a better job of hiding it.

Why Public Shaming Works

It makes sense to me that the sign treatment is a powerful lesson for a criminal. Even though we often consciously know that we're doing something wrong, even with smaller offenses that aren't illegal, it's easy for us to justify our actions in our own egocentric minds by saying that it's easy to get away with or that no one will go broke.

If we have to face our victims and feel empathy with the people we wronged, it's much more difficult to let ourselves off the hook. It probably has something to do with mankind's social nature. It's easy to steal from something abstract and lifeless like a store or even a person we'll never meet, but far more difficult to steal from a fellow human with feelings and desires like our own.

Thieves rarely return to the scene of the crime, but forcing them to confront the consequences of their actions has an interesting power to force shame on people, an extremely tricky feat by conventional means. You can't force someone in jail to have a realization about the consequences of hurting people, but forcing them into contact with the people they wronged can trigger these moments of self-reflection by making the impacts harder to avoid.

Furthermore, attacks on our reputations (or at least perceived attacks) are generally effective deterrent measures. Many game theorists see the concept of reputation as a society's way of solving the prisoner's dilemma, which is the idea that actions like cheating and stealing hurt society in the long term when everyone cheats and steals, but still seem appealing to individuals who stand to benefit in the short term. Even if it might financially benefit us to steal something, our society has convinced us that doing so causes others to look down on us, and that the damage to our reputations might outweigh the benefits of stealing.

Self-interested concern for our reputations is a strong motivator on its own that also gets lost when a criminal can escape the scene of the crime. A prison record certainly doesn't do one's reputation any favors, but the threat of a record is abstract and easy to forget about when deciding to break the law.

The Effect of Public Shaming

Carrying an embarrassing sign makes the damage unavoidable. Even if it doesn't hurt one's reputation as much as a black mark on a background check, public humiliation forces a person to see and feel the consequences very, very personally. If you think the damage to yourself is real, that makes it real.

Public shaming methods also have the added benefit of costing the taxpayers little money. In Putnam County, for example, Judge Miller gives his signature sign punishments in place of a 30-to-60-day jail sentence. Feeding and maintaining the imprisoned costs money (quite a lot of money at the national scale), and if there is an effective way to eliminate some of the cost with similar or better results, why not pursue it?

The old axiom "Let the punishment fit the crime" is still relevant, but it's a bit too narrow in scope. If you believe in the "debt to society" notion, an adequately sized punishment pays the criminal's debt and possibly deters other criminals, but it doesn't necessarily leave society any better afterward. A better axiom might be "Let the punishment fit the criminal."

> *"Punishments intended to shame offenders for wrongdoing, popular throughout history, are once again on the rise."*

Public Shaming Is Not a Good Substitute for Imprisonment

David M. Reutter

In the following viewpoint, David M. Reutter argues that public shaming is an unfair and inappropriate alternative to incarceration. While he appreciates the effort to avoid worsening the mass incarceration problem, Reutter contends that public shaming is an uneven approach to criminal justice that is often more about publicity than ensuring reform. Reutter is a contributor to Prison Legal News, *a monthly magazine published by the Human Rights Defense Center.*

As you read, consider the following questions:

1. According to Reutter, why do most judges embrace public shaming sentences?

2. According to Reutter, why has there been relatively little public backlash against public shaming?

3. According to Reutter, how might public shaming be socioeconomically biased?

Punishments intended to shame offenders for wrongdoing, popular throughout history, are once again on the rise—particularly as penalties imposed by judges who enjoy seeing their names in the newspaper or on television due to their "creative" sentencing practices.

Whether judges hand down sentences that humiliate defendants for the purpose of entertainment, self-aggrandizement or as a unique way of deterring crime with a "punishment that fits" is subject to debate. The only certainty is that most sanctions designed to shame offenders are legal, so long as judges do not go too far.

Public Shaming in History

Shaming criminals has long been an integral part of America's criminal justice system, and public whipping and the stocks were commonly used in Puritan and colonial times. During that era, imprisonment was reserved for debtors and those awaiting trial; upon conviction, a judge could order an offender to be executed, flogged, banished or shamed.

"While the sentences recognize hope for the individual, they can also be dehumanizing," said Professor Mark Osler of the St. Thomas University of Law.

Indeed, that was the intent of one colonial judge who sentenced a man convicted of stealing a pair of pants. The judge ordered him to sit in the stocks with "a pair of breeches about his necke." Public shaming sentences began to fade around the time of the American Revolution, though some shaming punishments, such as the pillory and branding for horse thieves, continued into the 1800s.

Urbanization and migration, say historians, undermined the use of public shaming because people no longer feared the condemnation of their communities. Imprisonment became the punishment of choice, yet states like Pennsylvania and Massachusetts still tried to shame prisoners by allowing the public to watch them "as if in a zoo."

Choosing Between Incarceration and Public Shaming

Some argue that the current system of incarcerating criminals and then releasing them on parole, or placing them on probation, is nothing more than a modern version of shaming. Critics of the criminal justice system contend that, like a yoke around the neck, criminal records follow former offenders forever, often preventing them from obtaining suitable employment, housing and public services.

"The purpose of incarceration ironically is to make someone feel ashamed at the end," said Peter Moskos, an associate professor of law and political science at the City University of New York, in a debate on shaming punishments that aired on National Public Radio (NPR) in August 2013. "We just have this horrible middle process to get someone there and we want people to feel shame and see what they did was wrong."

Moskos, who authored the book *In Defense of Flogging*, said the idea of humiliating punishments is to give people convicted of minor offenses an alternative to prison. "It's not that I want to see people whipped, but ... if you're sentenced to five years in prison for whatever you did or didn't do, and the judge gave you the choice of ten lashes, what would you pick?

"Almost everyone would choose the lashes, but we don't allow that because we consider it cruel and unusual. But if it's better than prison, what does that say about the system we have?" he concluded.

A Return to Flogging

Jonathan Turley, a professor of public interest law at George Washington University Law School, said during the NPR debate that he agrees that the current prison system is in need of reform but disagrees about shaming punishments.

"Let's reform our prisons. Let's focus on that," he stated. "But to say that we should go to a Singapore flogging system is breathtaking. We did that. We were there. We had flogging posts in [and] around our cities and towns. It was an extremely dark and medieval period."

Shaming punishments "have really undermined the quality and character of justice in this country," Turley added. "That is, it allows judges to become little Caesars that make citizens perform demeaning acts and shaming acts."

However, at least one state lawmaker thinks there's merit in public flogging. Montana Rep. Jerry O'Neil said he crafted legislation that would give convicted offenders the ability to choose between prison or the "infliction of physical pain."

"Ten years in prison or you could take 20 lashes, perhaps two lashes a year? What would you choose?" Rep. O'Neil said.

"It is actually more moral than we do now," he added. "I think it's immoral to put someone in prison for a long time, to take them away from their family, and force that family to go on welfare."

The idea was widely criticized by other Montana lawmakers and the American Civil Liberties Union, and O'Neil's bill, LC1452, died in committee in April 2013.

The Popularity of Public Shaming

The advent of mass media that seeks to entertain more than inform has contributed to the growing popularity of public shaming, and has helped some judges—who garner attention by imposing such sentences—become so popular that they have their own TV shows. For example, a Memphis judge allowed the victims of a theft to enter the thief's house and take anything they wanted as neighbors watched. The notoriety of that shaming sentence helped make Judge Joe Brown a household name for those who watch reality court TV.

The "King of Shame," Harris County, Texas, state judge Ted Poe, felt "people have too good a self-esteem." To bring defendants who appeared in his court down a rung, he would order them to do such things as shovel manure. While those punishments had little to do with justice, they did help Poe secure a congressional seat in 2004, and he remains in Congress today.

While studies show that shaming sentences are a poor deterrent to crime, the publicity surrounding such punishments makes them popular choices for judges who thrive on public attention. Then there are judges, such as Georgia's Russell "Rusty" Carlisle, who apparently enjoy humiliating people. When a littering defendant seemed "kind of cocky," Carlisle ordered him to use a butter knife to scrape gum off courtroom benches.

"The shaming punishments that we have seen are comical. They are ludicrous," Professor Turley noted. He said some judges ignore valid sentencing alternatives in order to seek notoriety. "It is a corruptive element in our judicial system and from what we've seen from judges is it's completely corrupting in terms of their own judgment and their own conduct," he stated. "They get worse and worse to get into the headlines."

Examples of Public Shaming

Judges have imposed a variety of shaming sentences in recent years, including:

- In November 2012, Shena Hardin, who was caught on camera passing a school bus by driving on a sidewalk, was ordered by Cleveland, Ohio, Municipal Court Judge Pinkey Carr to stand at an intersection wearing a sign that read, "Only an idiot would drive on the sidewalk to avoid a school bus." Similarly, in March 2013, Carr sentenced another defendant, Richard Dameron, who had threatened police officers, to stand outside a police station for three hours a day for one week with a sign apologizing to the officers and stating, "I was being an idiot and it will never happen again." Dameron failed to show up to hold the sign and was sentenced to 90 days in jail.

- In April 2014, Ohio Municipal Court Judge Gayle Williams-Byers ordered defendant Edmond Aviv to remain on a street corner for five hours with a sign that read, "I AM A BULLY! I pick on children that are disabled, and I am intolerant of those that are different from myself. My actions do not reflect an appreciation for the diverse South Euclid community that I live in." Aviv had pleaded no contest to disorderly conduct for harassing a neighboring family. "This isn't fair at all," he complained.

- A Georgia judge gave Natasha Freeman, 38, a choice of spending four weekends in jail or wearing a sign to resolve charges related to her boarding a school bus to assault her 11-year-old cousin. Freeman chose to wear a sign that said, "I made a fool out of myself on a Bibb County Public Schools bus," for one week, starting on December 10, 2012.

- In 2008, Cleveland, Ohio, Housing Court Judge Ray Pianka ordered landlord Nicholas Dionisopoulos to live in one of his own rental properties for six months after he was found in violation of multiple building codes. He also had to pay a $100,000 fine.

- In May 2012, a judge in Utah imposed the same punishment on two girls, 11 and 13, that they had inflicted on a 3-year-old girl they befriended at McDonald's. The older girls cut the little girl's hair into a bob with a pair of dollar store scissors. The judge sentenced the 13-year-old to detention and 276 hours of community service, but gave her the option to reduce the community service by more than half if she had her hair cut in the courtroom. She agreed. The 11-year-old was ordered to have her hair cut short at a salon.

- Two days before Christmas in 2013, Montana District Judge G. Todd Baugh ordered Pace Anthony Ferguson, 27, to write "Boys do not hit girls" 5,000 times as part of his punishment for punching his girlfriend. Ferguson was also ordered to serve six months in jail and pay $3,800 in medical bills for fracturing the woman's face in three places.

- In Pennsylvania, a prosecutor told two women to submit to public humiliation or face charges for stealing from a child. Evelyn Border, 55, and her daughter, Tina Griekspoor, 35, were caught taking a gift card from a girl at Walmart in 2009. They chose to stand in front of the courthouse holding signs that read, "I stole from a 9-year-old on her birthday! Don't steal or this could happen to you." The girl, Marissa Holland, reportedly said, "I think it's pretty fair. They deserved it. I want them to feel sorry."

- Daniel and Eloise Mireles, convicted of stealing from a victims' fund in Harris County, Texas, in 2010, were sentenced to a lengthy humiliating sentence. Along with jail terms, community service and restitution, the Mireleses were ordered by Judge Kevin Fine to hold signs saying, "I am a thief," at a busy intersection every weekend for six years. They also were required to post a sign in front of their house that included their names and said they were convicted thieves.

- A Wisconsin man who crashed his car into the gates of a wastewater treatment plant while drunk in 2008 was forced to choose between 20 days in jail for criminal damage to property or to stand at the plant for eight hours with a sign that said, "I was stupid." He chose the sign.

- After Jonathan Tarase pleaded no contest to DUI [driving under the influence of alcohol] in January 2013, Painesville, Ohio, Municipal Court Judge Michael Cicconetti, who is known for his unusual sentences, gave him a choice of either serving five days in jail or viewing the bodies of two victims killed in car accidents and taking a substance abuse course. In January 2014, Judge Cicconetti ordered Jeffrey Gregg to complete 400 hours of community service—while wearing a Santa Claus hat. Gregg's offense? He had posed as a Salvation Army bell ringer to collect money for himself. "It is too easy to put people in jail," Cicconetti said. "They go to jail and . . . it does not deter the crime."

The Public Shaming Trend

The above examples are in addition to more widespread public shaming of offenders both before they are convicted—such as booking mug shots posted by jails, and police websites that display photos of defendants arrested for soliciting prostitutes—and post-conviction shaming that includes sex offender registries, which have become ubiquitous.

Nor are modern shaming sentences a recent trend; in 2003, a Texas man was ordered to spend 30 consecutive nights in a 2-by-3 foot doghouse for whipping his stepson with a car antenna. The judge did allow Curtis Robin Sr. to have a sleeping bag, mosquito netting, plastic tarp or similar items during his stint in the doghouse. Other more recent sentences designed to shame or humiliate offenders have been reported since the 1990s.

Not all shaming sentences are legal or constitutional, though; some are questionable. For example, a 27-year-old Virginia man agreed in June 2014 to undergo a surgical vasec-

Public Shaming as Punishment

In America, our justice system is designed to be slow, methodical, a little boring. This is especially true in the sentencing phase. Even-tempered bureaucrats in bland black uniforms consult elaborately detailed guidelines to ensure that punishment is applied in consistent fashion across similar cases. . . .

Today, public shaming exercises haphazardly mix the real world with virtual reality. Judge Pinkey Carr sentences you to three hours of public sign-holding, but it's impossible to predict how many photos and videos the news media and random passersby may produce. Nor can you predict how much notice this imagery will attract. Maybe it will hit the Web but die with little fanfare. Maybe it will become a viral sensation.

Given that the whole point of public humiliation is to turn attention into punishment, an audience of one million is a more severe punishment than an audience of one thousand. What this means, effectively, is that when a judge orders a person to stand with a sign, or even when a police station publishes the mug shot of a prostitution client, they don't really know what degree of punishment they're sanctioning. . . .

Judges have the power to create their own unique sentences. And courts have ruled that sentences involving public shaming are constitutional as long as they aspire to some other goal, such as deterrence or retribution.

> *Greg Beato,*
> *"The Shame of Public Shaming,"*
> Reason, *July 2013.*

tomy in order to reduce his prison sentence for child endangerment, stemming from a vehicle accident that caused minor injuries to one of his children. "He needs to be able to support the children he already has when he gets out," said prosecutor Ilona White, who admitted the offer was intended to prevent Jessie Lee Herald from fathering more children than the seven he already had with at least six women.

"This takes on the appearance of social engineering," complained Richmond, Virginia, attorney Steve Benjamin, past president of the Virginia Association of Criminal Defense Lawyers. "Sentencing conditions are designed to prevent future criminal behavior," he said. "Fathering children is not criminal behavior."

Going to Extremes

In Oklahoma, District Court Judge Mike Norman ordered Tyler Alred, 17, to attend church for 10 years as a condition of his sentence for DUI manslaughter. Alred was behind the wheel of a pickup truck that crashed in December 2011, killing a passenger. The Oklahoma ACLU [American Civil Liberties Union] condemned the sentence, imposed in November 2012, as a "clear violation of the First Amendment," and filed a complaint against Norman. But the judge defended the punishment, which Alred had agreed to. Other conditions of the sentence included requirements that Alred graduate from high school, graduate from welding school, take drug and alcohol tests, and participate in victim impact panels.

Cameron County, Texas, Justice of the Peace Gustavo "Gus" Garza allowed parents to spank their children in his courtroom in lieu of paying a fine, for which he was admonished by the State Commission on Judicial Conduct on March 9, 2009. The commission concluded that "Judge Garza exceeded his authority by providing parents and the school district with a 'safe haven' for the administration of corporal punishment . . . with no legal authority to impose the sanction either by the Texas Education Code or Texas Code of Criminal Procedure."

And in Pennsylvania, in August 2014, a Superior Court struck down part of a shaming sentence imposed on former state Supreme Court justice Joan Orie Melvin, who was convicted of misusing public funds and using court and legislative staff to run her election campaigns. The trial court had ordered her to send pictures of herself wearing handcuffs to judges across the state; the Superior Court wrote that "the handcuffs as a prop is emblematic of the intent to humiliate Orie Melvin in the eyes of her former judicial colleagues. . . . It was solely intended to shame her."

"Judges have the power to create their own unique sentences. And courts have ruled that sentences involving public shaming are constitutional as long as they aspire to some other goal, such as deterrence or retribution," wrote *Reason* magazine contributing editor Greg Beato. "But equal application of the law is a crucial element of our justice system. It's one of the reasons we have sentencing guidelines. And quirky punishments designed to go viral don't just fail to meet this standard of the law; they actively subvert it. Their primary goal is to court publicity, and that publicity can't be accurately anticipated or controlled."

The Shame of Public Shaming

Experts say it stands to reason that so long as the public is entertained by shaming sentences, they will continue to be imposed. "These are punishments that often appeal to the public and bring a type of instant gratification for the court," said Professor Turley. "To some extent, we've seen the merging of law and entertainment in the last 10 years.

"Most of these people probably would not go to jail," he added. "People aren't taking a murderer and saying, 'I want you to bark like a dog in my courtroom and I'll let you off for murder.' These are relatively small offenses and many of them would not result in incarceration or weekend incarceration, but what these judges do is they impose very heavy sentences in order to force people to do what they want."

There may also be socioeconomic bias with respect to shaming sentences—when such punishments are offered as an option in lieu of fines, poor defendants are more inclined to choose them while wealthy offenders who can afford to pay financial penalties are less likely to submit to humiliating sanctions.

Unfortunately, many judges do not seem to understand that they can impose creative sentences that do not result in public shaming. For example, in December 2014, the *Detroit News* reported that Wayne County, Michigan, Circuit Court Judge Deborah Thomas, a former teacher, requires defendants to finish high school or obtain a GED [general equivalency diploma] certificate as part of their sentences. She posts the diplomas and certificates on her courtroom wall.

"Their job prospects are more limited, they have lower self-esteem," Thomas said of offenders who did not finish high school. "But when they have [the diploma] they have success, they realize 'I can succeed at other things.'" She added, "I tell them just because you came through here doesn't mean this has to be your permanent route.... We punish negative behavior. We should reward positive behavior."

Periodical and Internet Sources Bibliography

The following articles have been selected to supplement the diverse views presented in this chapter.

Greg Beato	"The Shame of Public Shaming," *Reason*, July 2013.
Matt Berman	"Can Public Shaming Be Good Criminal Punishment?," *National Journal*, September 9, 2013.
Jacob Jones	"Serving Electronic Time," *Inlander* (Spokane, WA), January 30, 2014.
James Kilgore	"Electronic Monitoring: Some Causes for Concern," *Prison Legal News*, March 15, 2012.
Patt Morrison	"Is Public Shaming Fair Punishment?," *Los Angeles Times*, May 24, 2014.
Brian Palmer	"Can We Bring Back the Stockades?," *Slate*, November 15, 2012.
Elaine Pawlowski	"Reevaluating Drug Courts: No Mother Should Have to Go Through What I Did," *Huffington Post*, July 29, 2013.
Mike Riggs	"Want to Go to Drug Court? Say Goodbye to Your Rights," *Reason*, August 17, 2012.
Maya Schenwar	"The Quiet Horrors of House Arrest, Electronic Monitoring, and Other Alternative Forms of Incarceration," *Mother Jones*, January 22, 2015.
Kim Soffen	"The Price of Electronic Prison," *Harvard Political Review*, July 14, 2014.
Sarah T. Williams	"Drug Courts in Minnesota: Smart on Crime, Not 'Soft on Crime,'" MinnPost, March 5, 2014.

For Further Discussion

Chapter 1

1. Michelle Alexander argues that the modern criminal justice system effectively functions like a racial caste system. What evidence does she provide to support this theory? Do you think this evidence is strong enough to support her hypothesis? Explain your answer.

2. As Jakub Wrzesniewski points out, Marie Gottschalk contends that American prisons are severely overcrowded because America has a cultural obsession with doling out punishment. Do you agree with this assertion? Why, or why not?

3. Brian Magee maintains that private prisons are detrimental to society because they value profit over the fair administration of justice. How does he justify his opinion? Does this seem like a valid argument? Explain.

Chapter 2

1. Jason L. Riley asserts that the high incarceration rate of African Americans is the result of the crime rate among African Americans. Do you agree with Riley, or do you think there is a better explanation for this phenomenon? Explain your answer.

2. Patricia O'Brien contends that America should stop incarcerating women and should shut down all women's prisons. Do you think this is a viable course of action? Why, or why not?

3. In her interview with Sara Mayeux, Nell Bernstein argues that incarceration is ineffective and often harmful for juvenile offenders. Why does she believe this? Do you agree with her argument? Why, or why not?

Chapter 3

1. Heather Rice asserts that subjecting prisoners to solitary confinement is torturous and immoral, while Greg Dobbs contends that it is a justified practice that still has a place in American prisons. Which of the two authors makes a more compelling, persuasive argument? Explain your answer.

2. Eliza Barclay reports that the use of nutraloaf as a dietary punishment is considered by some to be abusive, inhumane, and even unconstitutional. After reading the ingredients included in nutraloaf and the methods in which it is served, do you think using nutraloaf is a form of "cruel and unusual punishment," or do you think it is an effective deterrent for bad behavior of inmates? Explain your reasoning.

3. Jonathan Purtle argues that felon disenfranchisement has a direct effect on the health of African Americans. What evidence does he use to back up this claim? Is this evidence strong enough to support Purtle's conclusion? Explain your answer.

Chapter 4

1. Margaret Dooley-Sammuli and Nastassia Walsh contend that drug courts are not as beneficial as proponents such as Jessica Huseman claim. Do you agree with Dooley-Sammuli and Walsh's assessment? Why, or why not?

2. Dylan Matthews argues that electronic monitoring is a good way to keep people out of prison and addresses the mass incarceration problem. James Kilgore says that electronic monitoring is just as oppressive as incarceration. After reading both viewpoints, do you think electronic monitoring is an effective form of punishment? Explain your reasoning, citing text from the viewpoints to support your answer.

3. Brian Hampel advocates the use of public shaming sentences as an alternative to incarceration. Do you agree with Hampel's argument? Why, or why not? Would you accept a public shaming sentence if doing so meant avoiding a prison term? Explain your reasoning.

Organizations to Contact

The editors have compiled the following list of organizations concerned with the issues debated in this book. The descriptions are derived from materials provided by the organizations. All have publications or information available for interested readers. The list was compiled on the date of publication of the present volume; the information provided here may change. Be aware that many organizations take several weeks or longer to respond to inquiries, so allow as much time as possible.

American Civil Liberties Union (ACLU)
125 Broad Street, 18th Floor, New York, NY   10004
(212) 549-2500
website: www.aclu.org

Since 1920, the American Civil Liberties Union (ACLU) has worked to defend the civil liberties of American citizens. As part of its efforts, the ACLU regularly publishes materials on the Bill of Rights, including on prisoners' rights, in-depth reports such as "Banking on Bondage: Private Prisons and Mass Incarceration," and "Abuse of the Human Rights of Prisoners in the United States: Solitary Confinement." The ACLU also publishes the newsletter *Civil Liberties* and various handbooks on individual rights.

Amnesty International (AI)
5 Penn Plaza, New York, NY   10001
(212) 807-8400 • fax: (212) 627-1451
website: www.amnestyusa.org

Amnesty International (AI) is a worldwide organization that fights injustice and promotes human rights. Boasting more than 1.8 million members, AI is a global humanitarian organization dedicated to preserving and promoting human rights around the world. As part of these efforts, AI maintains an active news website and prepares special reports, such as "The

Edge of Endurance: Prison Conditions in California's Security Housing Units," on specific human rights issues. AI also publishes the *Wire,* a monthly magazine.

Brookings Institution

1775 Massachusetts Avenue NW, Washington, DC   20036

(202) 797-6000

e-mail: communications@brookings.edu

website: www.brookings.edu

Founded in 1927, the Brookings Institution is a sociopolitical think tank that conducts specialized research in foreign policy, government, economics, and other fields. Brookings also publishes papers such as "More Prisoners Versus More Crime Is the Wrong Question" and articles such as "How Digital Technology Can Reduce Prison Incarceration Rates." Its publications include the Policy Brief Series and the quarterly *Brookings Review.*

Center for Alternative Sentencing
and Employment Services (CASES)

151 Lawrence Street, 3rd Floor, Brooklyn, NY   11201

(212) 553-6300 • fax: (718) 596-3872

e-mail: info@cases.org

website: www.cases.org

The Center for Alternative Sentencing and Employment Services (CASES) is a criminal justice advocacy organization that stands opposed to the alleged overuse of incarceration as a form of criminal punishment. Over the course of its history, CASES has pioneered alternative sentencing programs in New York City, running the Court Employment Project, which provides felony offenders with intensive supervision and services, and founding the Community Service Sentencing Project, which provides support for repeat misdemeanor offenders. CASES also maintains an active online news archive and publishes various program brochures.

Corrections Connection Network News (Corrections.com)
15 Mill Wharf Plaza, Scituate, MA   02066
(617) 471-4445 • fax: (617) 608-9015
website: www.corrections.com

Corrections Connection Network News, better known as Corrections.com, is an online news source dedicated to improving national and international correctional policy and to promoting the professional development of corrections professionals. Since its inception in 1996, Corrections.com has made available a variety of books and correspondence courses on corrections and criminal justice. Its website offers an online database of corrections-related articles, including "The Importance of Cross-Gender Supervision."

Human Rights Watch (HRW)
350 Fifth Avenue, 34th Floor, New York, NY   10118-3299
(212) 290-4700 • fax: (212) 736-1300
website: www.hrw.org

Human Rights Watch (HRW) formed in 1988 when several large regional human rights organizations merged into a single global watchdog group. In support of its ongoing mission to promote the ethical treatment of people around the world, HRW publishes books, policy papers, and special reports, such as a 2013 report on the use of solitary confinement in juvenile detention facilities titled "Growing Up Locked Down." HRW sponsors an annual human rights film festival and takes legal action on behalf of individuals whose rights are violated.

National Center on Institutions and Alternatives (NCIA)
7222 Ambassador Road, Baltimore, MD   21244
(410) 265-1490 • fax: (410) 597-9656
website: www.ncianet.org

The National Center on Institutions and Alternatives (NCIA) is a criminal justice foundation that promotes community-based alternatives to prison that it believes better provide the education, training, and personal skills required for nonviolent offenders to be successfully rehabilitated and reintegrated into society. Through its efforts, NCIA seeks to help troubled individuals transform into productive, stable citizens. The NCIA website provides case studies, links to articles, and access to *Herb Hoelter's Criminal Justice Blog*, which features entries such as "Winning Lower Sentences over the Last 10 Years. Why?"

National Prison Project

915 Fifteenth Street NW, 7th Floor, Washington, DC   20005
(202) 393-4930 • fax: (202) 393-4931
website: www.aclu.org/prison

Formed by the American Civil Liberties Union (ACLU) in 1972, the National Prison Project provides resources and litigates cases with the aim of protecting and preserving criminal offenders' Eighth Amendment rights. Among other things, the project formally opposes practices such as electronic monitoring and the privatization of prisons. The project's publications include booklets such as the *Prisoners' Assistance Directory* and reports such as "A Death Before Dying" and "End the Abuse."

The Sentencing Project

1705 DeSales Street NW, 8th Floor, Washington, DC   20036
(202) 628-0871 • fax: (202) 628-1091
e-mail: staff@sentencingproject.org
website: www.sentencingproject.org

The Sentencing Project seeks to provide public defenders with sentence advocacy training so as to ensure that offenders might benefit from alternative sentences that lead to more positive and constructive outcomes than incarceration. In doing so, the Sentencing Project has increased public understanding of the sentencing process and the alternative sentencing programs currently available to offenders. The project publishes reports such as "Fewer Prisons, Less Crime" and "Ending Mass Incarceration: Social Interventions That Work."

US Department of Justice, Federal Bureau of Prisons (BOP)
320 First Street NW, Washington, DC   20534
(202) 307-3198
website: www.bop.gov

A subdivision of the US Department of Justice, the Federal Bureau of Prisons (BOP) oversees America's prison facilities and ensures public safety through the incarceration of dangerous criminals. Within its facilities, BOP seeks to provide work and other self-improvement opportunities to help offenders eventually make a seamless and productive return to society upon their prison release. BOP maintains an active online archive of news articles related to its operations and corrections in general, featuring titles such as "Institutions Prepare Inmates for Reentry" and "Paving the Way to a Successful Reentry."

Bibliography of Books

Michelle Alexander — *The New Jim Crow: Mass Incarceration in the Age of Colorblindness.* New York: The New Press, 2012.

Bryonn Bain — *The Ugly Side of Beautiful: Rethinking Race and Prison in America.* Chicago, IL: Third World Press, 2013.

Nell Bernstein — *Burning Down the House: The End of Juvenile Prison.* New York: The New Press, 2014.

Todd R. Clear and Natasha A. Frost — *The Punishment Imperative: The Rise and Failure of Mass Incarceration in America.* New York: New York University Press, 2014.

Ernest Drucker — *A Plague of Prisons: The Epidemiology of Mass Incarceration in America.* New York: The New Press, 2013.

Marie Gottschalk — *Caught: The Prison State and the Lockdown of American Politics.* Princeton, NJ: Princeton University Press, 2014.

Morris B. Hoffman — *The Punisher's Brain: The Evolution of Judge and Jury.* New York: Cambridge University Press, 2014.

Doran Larson, ed. — *Fourth City: Essays from the Prison in America.* East Lansing: Michigan State University Press, 2013.

Amy E. Lerman   *The Modern Prison Paradox: Politics, Punishment, and Social Community.* New York: Cambridge University Press, 2013.

Amy E. Lerman and Vesla M. Weaver   *Arresting Citizenship: The Democratic Consequences of American Crime Control.* Chicago, IL: Chicago University Press, 2014.

Mary D. Looman and John D. Carl   *A Country Called Prison: Mass Incarceration and the Making of a New Nation.* New York: Oxford University Press, 2015.

Melvin Mahone   *Prison Privatization in America: Costs and Benefits.* Seattle, WA: CreateSpace, 2012.

Marc Mauer and Sabrina Jones   *Race to Incarcerate: A Graphic Retelling.* New York: The New Press, 2013.

Deborah E. McDowell, Claudrena N. Harold, and Juan Battle, eds.   *The Punitive Turn: New Approaches to Race and Incarceration.* Charlottesville: University of Virginia Press, 2013.

Naomi Murakawa   *The First Civil Right: How Liberals Built Prison America.* New York: Oxford University Press, 2014.

Eugene Puryear   *Shackled and Chained: Mass Incarceration in Capitalist America.* San Francisco, CA: PSL Publications, 2013.

Steven Raphael and Michael A. Stoll — *Why Are So Many Americans in Prison?* New York: Russell Sage Foundation, 2013.

Beth Richie — *Arrested Justice: Black Women, Violence, and America's Prison Nation.* New York: New York University Press, 2012.

Maya Schenwar — *Locked Down, Locked Out: Why Prison Doesn't Work and How We Can Do Better.* Oakland, CA: Berrett-Koehler Publishers, 2014.

Jonathan Simon — *Mass Incarceration on Trial: A Remarkable Court Decision and the Future of Prisons in America.* New York: The New Press, 2014.

Jeff Smith — *Mr. Smith Goes to Prison: What My Year Behind Bars Taught Me About America's Prison Crisis.* New York: St. Martin's Press, 2015.

Ralph Spinelli — *Prison as Punishment.* Seattle, WA: CreateSpace, 2014.

Sara Wakefield and Christopher Wildeman — *Children of the Prison Boom: Mass Incarceration and the Future of American Inequality.* New York: Oxford University Press, 2014.

Kevin Wehr and Elyshia Aseltine — *Beyond the Prison Industrial Complex: Crime and Incarceration in the 21st Century.* New York: Routledge, 2013.

| John T. Whitehead, Kimberly D. Dodson, and Bradley D. Edwards | *Corrections: Exploring Crime, Punishment, and Justice in America.* 3rd ed. New York: Routledge, 2012. |
| Thomas Wills | *The Rise of America's Prisons: The War on the Poor.* Seattle, WA: CreateSpace, 2014. |

Index

F

Fabelo, Tony, 160
Fair Sentencing Act, 75
Fathi, David, 117
Federal Bureau of Investigation
(FBI), 71
Federal Bureau of Prisons (BOP)
avoidance of nutraloaf, 117
contract with private prisons,
47
difficulties created for women
prisoners, 75, 77
1930s establishment, 15–16
private prison contracts,
46–47
Second Chance Act authority,
78
techno-corrections debate, 160
Felon disenfranchisement
Congress's viewpoint, 127
Democratic/Republican viewpoint, 121–122
effects, 122–124
historical background, 127
impact on African Americans,
23, 120–123
Jim Crow laws similarity, 119,
120
mechanics, 120–122
positive aspects, 126
racist origins, 123
von Spakovsky's support, 125–
129
wrongfulness/dangerousness
of, 119–124
wrongness of activists against,
126–127
Fernandez, Angel, 149
Flatow, Nicole, 14
Flogging system, in Singapore, 169

Florida
Arthur G. Dozier School for
Boys, 85–86, 88
felon voting rights laws, 126
public shaming sentencing,
163, 165
Redirection Program, 88
2000 presidential election, 121
Florida Department of Correc-
tions, 126
Follow-on effects of mass incar-
ceration, 40–41
Food as punishment, 114–118
Fourteenth Amendment
(Constitution), 26, 127
Fourth Amendment
(Constitution), 25
Fraser, Aaron, 115
The French Connection film, 34
Friedmann, Alex, 64–65
Functional family therapy, 88, 94,
100

G

Gawande, Atul, 107
GEO Group, 47, 63, 157, 160
Geoghegan, Rory, 150
Goldsmith, Stephen, 55
Gore, Al, 121
Gottschalk, Marie
on change with dignity, de-
cency, 43–44
on emergence of mass incar-
ceration, 39–41
indictment of neoliberalism
by, 42
Governor's Office of Executive
Clemency (Florida), 126

felon disenfranchisement, 123
solitary confinement, 111
New Yorker article, 107
New Zealand, indigenous communities, 82
Newgate Prison (New York), 14
NIC. *See* National Institute of Corrections
Nixon, Richard, 34, 70–71
North Carolina, electronic monitor use, 154
North Korea, incarceration rate, 40
NRCAT. *See* National Religious Campaign Against Torture
Nutraloaf, as punishment, 114–118

O

Oakland, California, 21
Obama, Barack, 69, 154
O'Brien, Patricia, 79–83
Ohio
    prison overcrowding, 53, 54
    public shaming sentencing, 164
Oklahoma, prison overcrowding, 53
O'Neil, Jerry, 169
Osler, Mark, 167
Overcrowding in prisons, 18–19, 49, 52–54, 78
Owen, Steve, 63

P

Palta, Rina, 61–67
Panic in Needle Park film, 34
Parole
    African American rate, 22

disenfranchisement effect, 120–121
electronic monitoring adjunct, 147, 156
Rockefeller drug laws impact, 33
Truthout parolee interviews, 156
Patient Protection and Affordable Care Act (Obamacare), 122–123
Patterson, Craig, 160
Pelchat, Marcia, 116
Pennsylvania, use of nutraloaf, 115–116
Persico, Joseph, 33, 34, 37
Petrella, Christopher, 62–64, 66
Physical abuse, 59, 76, 85, 95, 103, 146, 149
Policy Exchange think tank, 150
Powe, Lucas A., Jr., 70
Prison Divestment Campaign (2011), 49–50
Prison guards unions, 42, 46
Prison system (public prisons)
    drug arrest data, 23–24
    dysfunctionality, cruelty in, 45–50
    New Deal reforms, 16
    overrepresentation of African Americans, 61–67
    post-Civil War evolution of, 15
    punishment vs. rehabilitation focus, 15
    reasons for design of, 59–60
    state spending on, 81
    Turley's opinion on, 168–169
    2007, U.S. spending, 140
    war on drugs impact on, 32–37